Sahir

Sahir

A Literary Portrait

Surinder Deol

OXFORD
UNIVERSITY PRESS

OXFORD
UNIVERSITY PRESS

Oxford University Press is a department of the University of Oxford.
It furthers the University's objective of excellence in research, scholarship,
and education by publishing worldwide. Oxford is a registered trademark of
Oxford University Press in the UK and in certain other countries.

Published in India by
Oxford University Press
22 Workspace, 2nd Floor, 1/22 Asaf Ali Road, New Delhi 110 002

ISBN-13 (print edition): 978-0-19-949905-2
ISBN-10 (print edition): 0-19-949905-5

ISBN-13 (eBook): 978-0-19-909838-5
ISBN-10 (eBook): 0-19-909838-7

Typeset in Minion Pro 10.5/13.5
by Tranistics Data Technologies, Kolkata 700 091
Printed in India by Replika Press Pvt. Ltd

Poetry is a deep inner calling in man; from it came liturgy, the psalms, and also the contents of religions. The poet confronted nature's phenomena and in the early ages called himself a priest, to safeguard his vocation ... Today's social poet is still a member of the earliest order of priests. In the old days he made his pact with the darkness, and now he must interpret the light.

Pablo Neruda
Memoirs

Publisher's Note

Every effort has been made to contact the copyright holders, some of whom could not be identified or located. Any information brought to notice regarding these copyright holders will be acknowledged in future reprints of the book.

Oxford University Press India would like to thank Mr Amar Nath Verma, Chairman, Star Publications (P) Ltd, for his wonderful stories about Sahir Ludhianvi and for granting permission to reproduce his poetry.

Contents

Foreword

When we want to write about Sahir, we face a dilemma: where do we start—and how do we bring a conversation about him to a fruitful conclusion? Nearly 40 years have passed since his death, but his poetry—set to music by some of the best music directors of our time—never fails to connect with our deep-seated emotions and longings. Sahir made his mark as a literary star in the 1940s, when there was no dearth of highly talented romantic or revolutionary poets, dazzling everyone with his talent. That could be a good starting point. Or we could talk about how he birthed a new kind of songwriter, one who redefined what it meant to be a film lyricist—not an unknown presence behind the scenes, but one who enjoyed celebrity status on his own terms.

It has been reported in the press that Sahir is going to be the subject of a Bollywood biopic. Why didn't someone think of that before? Millions of people who don't know the poet would get a chance to be mesmerized by the lyricism of his words.

Sahir had a fractured educational career. As a high schooler, he attended a Sikh denominational school. So though he didn't know much about Islam, the religion of his parents, he learnt a lot about Sikhism. He also learnt how to write a poem or a *ghazal* in Urdu here, because of the instruction he received from one of his teachers. And then there were disruptions. It is not clear whether he was expelled from Government College in Ludhiana or he left it on his own. He never earned the degree that he aspired to, despite attending two other colleges in Lahore. But in the larger scheme of things, he didn't attach much importance to this lack.

Attending mushairas was a craze for the younger generation at that time. Imagine Sahir getting on the stage. The hall is filled with young students who cheer each line that he speaks with cries of '*mukarrar!*' And when he recites his best poem, '*Taj Mahal*', he wins the hearts and minds of his audience many times over. There's always a long queue of students—male and female—wanting his autograph.

At a public event in Lahore where Sahir read '*Taj Mahal*', there was a slim, delicate, and extremely beautiful young girl who stood at the end of the queue. When it was her turn for an autograph, she extended her hand instead of the customary notebook. Sahir took a pen and wrote on her palm, 'I have signed a blank cheque. You can cash it any time.'

Long before this event, there was another mushaira about which Kanhaiya Lal Kapoor has written—held in Lahore's Government College.[1] This was the time when the wave the of the Progressive Writers' Movement, led by Sajjad Zaheer, was at its peak. A senior poet, Ehsan Danish, was presiding. Josh Malihabadi was also on the stage. At the start of the event, an unknown young poet was asked to recite his work. The poet got up from one of the back rows and climbed the stage. He recited just one poem—'*Mujh Se Pehli Si Muhabbat Mere Mahbuub N Maang*'. There were cheers, but the young poet, unconcerned about the applause, quickly disappeared into the crowd. Others came and read their work, but the one who had caused the commotion was nowhere to be seen. That was Faiz Ahmed Faiz, and the poem was part of Faiz's first anthology, *Naqsh-e Fariyaadi*. In the same way, *Talkhiyaan*, Sahir's first poetical collection, had '*Taj Mahal*' as the key thematic poem. Both these volumes are treasures of modern Urdu poetry and they have appeared in several anthologies of the poets' works and of Urdu poetry.

I mention these incidents and these poetical volumes to highlight the fact that these two poems point to the differences between

[1] Kanhaiya Lal Kapoor, '*Phir Nazar Mein Phool Mehke*', in S. Taqi Abedi (ed.), *Faiz Fahmi* (Lahore: Reconer Publications, 2011), 953–5.

these young poets and their creativity. Faiz's work featured a highly innovative fusion of romanticism with a strong flavour of revolutionary thinking and deep empathy for the downtrodden, along with distinctive similes and metaphors that were new to Urdu poetry. His poetic artistry reached new heights as he struggled with oppression and the forces that wanted to silence his voice. Sahir, in a way, bid adieu to the political revolution to which progressive poets like Faiz were deeply committed and joined the film industry. But to his credit, he never stopped writing about social injustice, about the sufferings of the poor and the victims of oppression. The differences between these two poets are puzzling and they do not lend themselves to easy explanations.

As I talk about Sahir, I cannot stop thinking about my first meeting with him—it happened in a location known for many historical twists and turns. Let me explain. After the events of 1857, Delhi as a city was devastated. There was a new world that was about to be born. The British rulers cleared the area surrounding Red Fort and thus destroyed some historic alleys—iconic streets and neighbourhoods we associate with poets like Mir and Ghalib. Similarly, nothing much was left around Jama Masjid. But, in due course, life resumed. The shopkeepers returned. The new attraction was Victoria Park, and it had a statue of Queen Victoria glamorously riding a horse. After Independence, poet Naresh Kumar Shad remarked that it was easy for the queen to get on horseback, but a lot of effort was required to bring her down to earth.

When the Urdu writer and revolutionary Sajjad Zaheer returned from Pakistan after his imprisonment there (around 1954–5), I met him in Victoria Park. It was a shortcut if you were going to Urdu Bazaar. Just in front of the park thrived this magnificent world of Urdu literature and literary journalism. There were numerous bookstores selling Urdu books. There was Maktaba Jamia Limited, Kutub Khana Anjuman-e Taraqqi-e Urdu (Hind), and offices of *Shaahraah*, the progressive monthly magazine. Around the corner, there was Maktaba-e Burhan, and Hali Publishing House where Shahid Ahmad Dehlvi edited the famous magazine *Saqi*. A large number of people visited these places, and the evenings especially were filled with writers and their friends enjoying books of Urdu poetry and prose while tasting kebabs and sipping cups of tea. Everyone who passed through this area would stop at Maulvi Samiillah Khan's. By then, I had earned my MA degree and was working on my doctoral dissertation. I would go to the University on a motorbike, and most days, riding pillion was my friend Nisar Ahmed Faruqi, who worked in the University library. We made it a point to stop at the Maulvi's. An added attraction used to be the generosity of Shahid Bhai of Maktaba Jamia who would allow us to browse books that we didn't have money to buy.

One such day in the early 1950s, I was sipping tea and indulging in small talk with my friends when I saw a tall, handsome young man carrying some papers and magazines approach us. This was Sahir Ludhianvi. His book *Talkhiyaan* was already the talk of the town. He had earned fame at an early age. There was an attention-grabbing sparkle in his eyes. We got up, shook hands, and introduced ourselves. He was continuously inhaling and puffing out cigarette smoke. The magazine that he carried with him was his new venture, *Shaahkaar.* We talked for some time and he got our promise to write for his magazine, and then he left us in a hurry, disappearing into the crowd. Soon after this meeting, I came to know that Sahir had gone to Bombay to try his luck in films. Success came to him early on. Though *Shaahraah,* where Sahir had worked before, shut down, and *Shaahkar* also collapsed after one or two issues, the promising literary poet had successfully turned himself into a film lyric poet. When *Pyaasa* was released in the late 1950s, Sahir had reached the peak of his popularity. Even Prime Minister Nehru appreciated his poem, '*Jinhein naaz hai Hind par voh kahaan hain*', that was at the very heart of this film. Sahir was no longer the same man I had once met. This was a new Sahir—highly self-conscious, somewhat narcissistic, and dismissive of others' work and talents. This new attitude cost him friendships: music director S.D. Burman, who played a crucial role in making Sahir a successful lyricist, stopped working with him. There were others too, and I don't wish to go into these details.

Sahir's enigmatic personality had many shades. I met him twice in Bombay along with his bosom buddy, Sabar Dutt, who was running a periodical devoted mainly to special issues. I had helped Dutt in the preparation of special issues of his magazine on Mohinder Nath, Kamleshwar, Faiz, etc. Later on, I worked with him to organize a special issue on Sahir's life and work.

By then Sahir had achieved such success that he could tell the film director who should be the music director transforming his words into musical scores. No poet had ever commanded that kind of control. This happened when there were other highly accomplished poets and writers—such as Ali Sardar Jafri, Jan Nisar Akhtar, Akhtar Ul Iman, Ismat Chughtai, Krishan Chander, and Rajinder Singh Bedi—who were also writing for films. While these people struggled to pay their rents, Sahir built an impressive seaside mansion named after one of his poems.

Once when I was visiting Bombay, I got a message through Sabar Dutt that I should visit Sahir one of the evenings. This was when Sahir had moved away from the literary world, focusing all his attention on film songs. His last important literary creation was a long poem titled 'Parchhaaiyan', a poem about war and peace. As he stopped creating new literary jewels, he started to rehash some of his best work to suit the needs of films. A classic example is the poem 'Kabhi Kabhi' from Talkhiyaan that he partially rewrote for use in Yash Chopra's film of the same title. The progressive poets whom Sahir had left behind were now chiding him: Is socialism all for one's own success? What happened to the dreams of a political revolution that was the very foundation of your work? Some of them even quoted the punchline from his poem 'Taj Mahal': 'Ik shahanshaah ne daulat ka sahaara le kar/ham ghariibon ki mohabbat ka uraaya hai mazaaq.' In fact, this was the story of many progressive writers who met with success and became part of the establishment. Famous novelist Qurratulain Hyder, who in earlier days was a victim of Ismat Chughtai's sarcasm, wrote Aakhir-e Shab Ke Ham Safar, her most successful novel, for which she was felicitated with the Jnanpith Award. The book dealt with how revolutionaries of yesteryears become the worst opportunists, or how a revolution eventually eats its own children.

I want to go back to my meeting with Sahir. His welcome was filled with lots of love. He brought out a bottle of expensive Scotch. We sat on the fancy woodcut porch on the second floor, looking at the ocean in its moonlit splendour, breathing in the fresh air while talking about things of common interest. I do not remember anything significant that came out of that meeting. There was a second meeting and again not very consequential in any way.

Let me say a few words about the romantic side of Sahir's enigmatic life. And that is his 'relationship' with path-breaking Punjabi poet, novelist, and essayist Amrita Pritam, whose hand Sahir had autographed years ago. These two exceptionally talented authors and their stories are strangely intermingled and they continue to fascinate fans several decades after they have passed on. Amrita Pritam had no ambition to be a great writer, but then Partition happened and millions of lives were shattered and destroyed. She was a witness to horrific brutalities and her soul was crushed with the weight of the beastliness of human beings on both sides of the border. The tragedy was severe and much deeper for women, who were victimized in the most degrading ways possible. In a soulful cry, Amrita, the raw young voice of Punjabi poetry, reached out to the great Punjabi Sufi seer and poet Waris Shah, creator of the classic folk tale 'Heer Ranjha', who had died centuries ago. She begged him to speak out from his grave, telling him that he had written a great mournful masterpiece on the tragic love story of one daughter of Punjab, Heer, but now there were millions of young girls and women who were victims of heart-chilling atrocities: Why not rise from your grave and say something to these sufferers of heart-rending indignities?

ajj aakhaan Waris Shah nuun
k tuun qabraan vich-chon bol

te ajj kitaab-e i'shq da
koi agla varqa phol

This was such a powerful poem that it captured the attention of the entire young generation of migrants and was translated into many Indian languages. This was Amrita Pritam's answer to Sahir's '*Taj Mahal*'.

I have a vivid recollection of Amrita receiving the Sahitya Akademi award from Prime Minister Nehru, in a sari and a necklace of white pearls that had the shine of her poetic genius. She was doing great writing, but her day job (reading Punjabi news at All India Radio) was not that interesting. When she published her shockingly candid autobiography, *Rasidi Ticket*, her fascination for Sahir was no longer a secret. She wrote about it in great detail. The shock of unrequited love was one thing, but Amrita faced many other challenges. Several Hindi and Punjabi writers were irked by her phenomenal literary success, and that included influential Punjabi writer Kartar Singh Duggal, who lived in a big bungalow a few yards away from Amrita's small house in Hauz Khas. Sipping their evening Scotch, Duggal and many of his friends would declare that they would never let Amrita win the prestigious Jnanpith Award. But public opinion worked in her favour and a time came when she was rightly chosen for that unique honour. In all these developments, Sahir's enigmatic image was always in the background, a lover who was present in his absence—maybe a source of wounded inspiration, or just a fleeting companion of her dreams, whose memory was deep and was dripping blood.

Amrita's enemies didn't let her lead a restful life. She wrote a novella titled *Hardit ka Zindagi Nama*, but the *Zindagi Nama* title had been used earlier by well-known Hindi writer Krishna Sobti for her autobiography. Opportunist writers like Namwar Singh and Ashok Bajpai instigated Sobti to sue Amrita for copyright infringement. Consequently, a case was filed against Amrita by Sobti's publisher in Bhopal. This was a frivolous case that should have been dismissed after one hearing. But that is not how the judicial system in India works.

This was the time when Amrita had legally separated from her husband and was living with an artist named Imroze, whose pencil sketches for the most popular *Sham'a* magazine reflected different shades of Amrita's beautiful face and figure. They lived in my neighbourhood. I often met the couple when my wife Manorma and I went with our son Tarun for his soccer practice in a nearby park. One day, Amrita came to my home visibly distraught. We talked about the copyright infringement case. I told her that '*zindagi nama*' was a generic Urdu and Persian word and thus it could not be copyrighted. She asked me to research the origin and usage of the word. I promised her my full support and we submitted extensive documentation and asked the court to dismiss this case in the first hearing. But, unfortunately, while the judge was highly incompetent, he was relishing the attention from the press, and thus the case dragged on for 10–12 years.

It is important to clarify that until then Amrita's relationship with Imroze was a working—and not a romantic—one. She was in love with only one person, and that was Sahir. One time, she went to Bombay and Imroze accompanied her. She met Sahir several times. Every time she opened herself to him, she reached a dead end. She heard rumours that Sahir was having an affair with singer Sudha Malhotra, a rumour that was denied by Ms Malhotra several times in later years. Amrita returned to Delhi with a broken heart.

The last time I saw Amrita was when, as president of Sahitya Akademi, I nominated her for the prestigious Akademi Fellowship on the occasion of the institution's golden jubilee celebrations, and this honour was conferred on her by Prime Minister Manmohan Singh. Amrita had lost her youthful persona by then; she was frail, almost a bundle of bones. But there were some things that time had not taken away from her: the sparkle in her eyes and the speech filled with passion and wisdom. Now, when Sahir and Amrita are no longer with us, the twisted contours of their relationship continue to cast a long shadow, and this mystery of love and its enigmatic nature is unlikely to ever be fully resolved.

For a poet, it is always a difficult challenge to separate different segments of their literary output. Akhtar Ul Iman, who was a great literary poet, limited his role in films to a dialogue writer. He never allowed his poetry to be used in films. Gulzar has been very successful in separating his literary life from his film life. Javed Akhtar, who came to films as a scriptwriter, gave up scriptwriting when he was accepted as a film lyricist. Sahir made a choice and gave up on his literary life, which is sad because there was a lot more left to say. Sahir insisted in several interviews that film work was not only literary work, it was even more potent, because film lyrics reached millions of people who do not read literature in any form. To what extent that point of view is valid, I leave to the judgement of the readers, but as a literary critic, I do see a gap that is difficult to fill.

In conclusion, let me say something about the author of this literary biography. I met Surinder Deol after he had published his free-verse translation of *Divan-e Ghalib*, titled *The Treasure*.[2] I was so impressed by the quality of his work that I accepted his invitation to be the chief guest at the book launch ceremony held in Washington, DC, in the summer of 2014. Our meetings increased in the following months, and looking at Surinder's ability to masterfully unlock the mystery of Mirza's poetic masterpiece in a language that was simple and yet filled with great artistry and lyricism, I asked him to work with me to translate my Urdu book on Ghalib that had been published by the Sahitya Akademi.[3] It took us about three years to complete this task, and the fruits of our collaboration are now in public view.[4] Surinder fell in love with Sahir's poetry while he was a college student. His understanding of Sahir matured with time and, as you read his rendering of Sahir's *nazms* and ghazals, you will be struck by the effortless flow of words, like the slow passage of water in a stream; once you put your hand into it, you don't feel like moving away. Sahir

---

[2] Surinder Deol, *The Treasure: A Modern Rendition of Ghalib's Lyrical Love Poetry* (New Delhi: Partridge Publishing, 2018, 2nd ed).

[3] Gopi Chand Narang, *Ghalib: Ma'ni Aafrini Jadilyati Vaza' Shunyata aur Sheriyaat* (New Delhi: Sahitya Akademi, 2014).

[4] Gopi Chand Narang, *Ghalib: Innovative Meanings and the Ingenious Mind*, trans. Surinder Deol (New Delhi: Oxford University Press, 2017).

is a major Urdu poet and yet there is no good translation of his work. I am confident that this book will be widely read, and all those who love good literature will be entranced and bedazzled by Surinder's exposition of Sahir's life and his poetic work.

Gopi Chand Narang*

---

* Professor Gopi Chand Narang, a former president of Sahitya Akademi, has won global recognition for his outstanding contribution to literature. He has received the Sitara-e Imtiaz (2012) and the President's Gold Medal from Pakistan, and the Padma Shri (1990), the Sahitya Akademi Award (1995), and the Padma Bhushan (2004) from India. He has received D.Litt. (Honoris Causa) from the Central University of Hyderabad (2007), Aligarh Muslim University (2009), and Maulana Azad National University, Hyderabad (2012). He has been bestowed the rare honour of Professor Emeritus by the University of Delhi and the Jamia Millia Islamia university.

Preface
A Mystery Wrapped in an Enigma

duniya ne tajarbaat v havaadis ki shakl mein
jo kuchh mujhe diya hai vo lauta raha huun main

Whatever the world gave me
in the shape of experiences and calamities,
I'm giving it back.

—Sahir Ludhianvi

Soon after he started writing for films, sometime around 1950, Sahir ceased to be an ordinary Urdu poet; he became a celebrity. At the peak of his popularity, he was just like any other film star—amply photographed and the subject of stories and speculations in film magazines. Because of this, we can surmise that his life remained very much in public view and we know everything that was important to know about him. This, however, is not the case. Despite media exposure, Sahir remains a mystery up to this day. We do not have answers to many questions pertaining to his private life, public persona, and even his poetry. Psychologists point out that children who grow up in the care of a single mother (who is also financially strained) carry with them the burden of insecurity all their life. Love for the mother can often eliminate the need for love for any other woman. Does this explain Sahir's numerous affairs which never got anywhere? We can't say with any certainty.

Sahir entered the literary world like a storm, and soon thereafter he was appointed editor of a prestigious Urdu magazine. But no sooner did he achieve success as a film lyricist, he began to keep the literary world at a distance. He rarely participated in mushairas and other literary activities. Sahir started his life with a large circle of friends, but as time passed, he narrowed this circle to such an extent that the day his body was carried for burial, after sudden death from a heart attack, there were only a handful of friends present on his last journey. Did this have anything to do with behavioural issues, or excessive drinking, or the bouts of depression that he complained about? We do not have a clear answer to this question, but a good place to start is his life story and his assertion that he was simply giving back in words the wounds his own life had inflicted on him.

Sahir was born on 8 March 1921 to a wealthy, land-owning family in a village near Ludhiana, an industrial town in eastern Punjab not particularly known for producing literary geniuses like other Punjab towns such as Lahore. He was given the Koranic name Abdul Hayee. It was a matter of great celebration for his father, Chaudhri Fazl Mohammad, who had married ten times before but had been blessed with a child for the first time. Sahir's mother was his eleventh wife. Fazl Mohammad had all the bad habits of spoilt landlords: unabashed exploitation of farm workers and farmers, arrogance founded on ignorance, and a decadent lifestyle sustained by heavy borrowing. Sahir's mother, Sardar Begum, a charming, self-confident woman of Kashmiri descent, tolerated the excesses of her husband for several years, but when Sahir was about three or four years old, she took the bold step of leaving her husband. She moved to Ludhiana city and started a new life with support from her brother, Abdul Rashid.

As Sahir was very young when he was taken away from his father's home, he carried vague impressions of his childhood. There was one image, however, that recurred for many years. It was that of a vast haveli built with Mughal-style red bricks. He ruminated about his ancestors in the following words.

I belong to ancestors
who have supported an alien regime
like their own shadow.
From their sinful role in the mutiny
they stood by their foreign masters
at every difficult point in time.

While his father thought that only children of poor families needed to be educated to get a job, and the son of a landlord could lead an opulent life without ever going to school, Sahir's mother saw a future for her son that relied solely on the basis of the education he received. It never crossed her mind that her son would earn fame and money by being a poet. The father did not reconcile himself with the new reality and initiated a legal custody battle that lasted several years. Sardar Begum eventually prevailed because young Sahir told the judge unequivocally that he wanted to live in the sole custody of his mother. The judge was also influenced by the fact that while the mother wanted her son to get an education, the father claimed that education for a landlord's son was a waste of time. As the custody battle came to an end, Chaudhri didn't wait much longer to marry a twelfth time. Sahir wrote several poems bemoaning the idle and lecherous lifestyle of landlords like his own father. Look at these lines from his poem 'Jaagiir'.

Their toil is mine
and the fruit of their labour
is mine too
Their arms are mine
and so too
the produce of these arms.
I am the lord of this inheritance
without any question.
The pleasure of these cheeks
and the breeze of these tresses—
they belong to me.

As a child, Sahir was very interested in books, even books by poets like Allama Iqbal, which were beyond his understanding. He would force his maternal uncle to buy these books and read certain passages to him. When he got admitted to a Sikh denominational high school, he found a good teacher, named Faiyaz Haryanvi, who helped Sahir to get a good grip over Urdu and Persian. In fact, it was this teacher who commented on the very first poem that Sahir wrote. It was a conditional appreciation: technically perfect, but not much depth. This made Sahir happy because he was afraid that he would never understand the technique of writing poetry.

As is the common practice among Urdu poets, their life's creative work starts with choosing a *takhallus*. In the summer of 1937, Sahir came across a poem that Allama Iqbal wrote in praise of poet Dagh Dehlvi. The following couplet took his breath away:

is chaman mein honge paida bulbul-e shiraaz bhi
sainkron saahir bhi honge saahib-e e'jaaz bhi

In this garden of poesy shall be born
poets like the nightingale of Shiraz.[1]
There shall be numerous magicians
and persons with miraculous abilities.

It took only a few moments for him to select 'Sahir' (sorcerer, wizard, enchanter, illusionist, mentalist, and magician) as his takhallus, and thus a foundation stone for the eventual blossoming of a great poet was laid.

The ghazals Sahir wrote during his school years were simplistic, but they showed potential. Here are a few samples:

Don't worry about me.
I spit blood when I cough.
The lamp of my life is about to die out.
It is flickering.

Enjoy these days—
Relish the pleasures
that youth brings.

---

[1] The great Persian poet Hafiz or Hafez (1315–1390) was known as the Nightingale of Shiraz.

Let me go.
Revolution is waiting for me.
It is about to surface—
the sun of a new age.

Enrolling in the city's prestigious Government College marked the start of a tumultuous phase of Sahir's life—with several others to follow. Sahir was now writing better poetry, and his fame was spreading around town. He was chosen president of the student's union, a forum he used to express his anti-British and pro-independence feelings. This brought him to the notice of the college principal, who was British, and of the district law enforcement authorities. But he had to leave the college without getting a degree, under circumstances that are not clear. In frustration, he left Ludhiana in 1941 and took a train to Lahore, which was then the centre of most artistic and literary activities in north India. It is interesting that while the college did not value Sahir's talent when he was a student, the injustice done under British rule was redressed in 1970 when the college management invited him back and honoured him with a gold medal that was presented by V.K.R.V. Rao, who was minister of education at that time.

Once he was socially and economically secure, Sahir came under considerable pressure from his mother to get married. On this topic, he had a stock answer that he gave his mother and others:

I am not against the institution of marriage, but I have not felt the need to get married. There are many dimensions to man–woman relationships. It should not be limited to a husband and wife relationship. Your love for your mother and sister is equally important. I have two younger sisters and I love them a lot. This indirectly satisfies my need to be a parent.[2]

Ahmad Rahi, who was Sahir's close friend during his stay in Lahore, summed up the reason for Sahir's inability to bring any romantic

---

[2] Balwant Singh, 'Ham Ke Thahre Ajnabi', Fan aur Shakhsiat, 17–18, 1985: 50.

relationship to fruition. 'People say that Sahir fell in love many times. I don't agree with this assessment. In his entire life, Sahir loved once and he nurtured one hate. He *loved* his mother and he *hated* his father' [Emphasis added].[3]

Because Sahir did not have a normal childhood, he suffered from insecurity. He had seen how his mother raised him in the face of severe constraints, financial and otherwise. Thus, it is likely that he lacked the confidence required for establishing a strong personal relationship. Until 1976, when his mother passed away, he did not want any other woman to be part of his life. That is why the death of his mother had such a devastating impact on Sahir. According to film director Yash Chopra, 'After his mother's death, he went into a shell. He would say "I am not enjoying writing any more." His loneliness must have killed him.'[4]

Based on the accounts of his friends, Sahir was an introvert who enjoyed smoking and drinking in the company of a few close friends. One possible explanation could be a fear that once he got married he would be required to change his lifestyle, and the birth of one or more kids would totally change the arc of his life. To this a psychologist might add that men of high artistic calibre are sometimes not prepared to carry the burden of a strong personal relationship within the confines of a traditional marriage. They look upon it as a constraint and are afraid of the failure that a broken marriage brings. On the other hand, the persona of one suffering from unrequited love, of a tragic lover, is potentially a great asset to project to those who consume the artist's output, whether book or painting. Sahir was incapable of giving happiness to any woman in a lifelong relationship. All these stories about his romances were nothing more than an aid to strengthening his celebrity status. There is no evidence that he regretted this free publicity.

[3] Ahmad Rahi, '*Ek Diya Aur Bujha*', *Adab Saaz*, 12–14, 2010: 54.

[4] Akshay Manwani, *Sahir Ludhianvi: The People's Poet* (Delhi: HarperCollins, 2013) Kindle edition, Ch. 13.

We may call it complexity or mystery. Sahir was a human being after all, and like all of us, he showed complications and intricacies in his life that we often exhibit. In the words of his friend Mohinder Nath:

> Sahir is a bundle of contradictions. He is a mixture of good and bad. He is famous as well as notorious. He is a fountain of much good and a big pile of personal shortcomings. In reality, every man is internally a confluence of light and darkness. If a man is all good, then he cannot be a man; he becomes an angel. All said, Sahir is a sincere man and he is filled with much goodness.[5]

The unknown poet who used to wander the streets of Ludhiana at night in the company of a few of his close friends achieved fame as a poet and film lyricist that was beyond anyone's expectation. One day, he exited this world suddenly, without much fanfare. His cousin Anwar Sultana talked about his last days:

> Bhaijan was heartbroken after Ma-ji's death. Then he suffered a heart attack and that changed his routine. He started to eat his food alone in his room. Sometimes at dinner he would address me ... 'Look, Anwar, I tried to help you and the family financially so that you don't suffer ... One thing I can tell you is that you will rarely find good people who will truly protect you. It is not because the world is devoid of good and sincere folk. The problem is that their numbers are limited.' When he talked like this it made me very sad. I told him that I wouldn't like to listen to these things: 'You're going to live very long.' But deep down Bhaijan knew that his days in this world were numbered ... Eventually, the ill-fated day of 25 October 1980 arrived when I took him to Dr Kapoor's place. He was alright and was talking with Dr Kapoor in a normal manner. Suddenly, his neck fell on one side and he was silenced for good. We were hit by lightning. No one can fathom our pain and suffering.[6]

---

[5] Mohinder Nath, 'Sahir Ba-Hasiyat Dost aur Shaa'yir', Fan aur Shakhsiat, 17–18, 1985: 86.

[6] Mahmud Ayubi, 'Anwar Bibi Ke Bhaijan', Fan aur Shakhsiyat, 17–18, 1985: 46.

Sahir was buried at the Juhu Muslim cemetery, but in 2010 the remains of all those who were buried there were removed to make room for new interments. Sadly, it reminds us of one of Mirza Ghalib's famous couplets:

Why didn't I drown myself in a river
to avoid notoriety?
It would have saved a coffin,
a grave, and a tombstone.[7]

An Iconic Literary Poet

We can call Sahir a wizard of 'bittersweet' melodies, borrowing a phrase from the title of his first poetry collection. Whether he wrote a poem or a ghazal, he packaged it like a piece of confection (i.e., romance), but underneath that sweetness he camouflaged bitterness (i.e., oppression, income inequality, exploitation), shocking his reader's sensibility.

In his early years, Sahir was influenced by poets like Allama Iqbal, Josh Malihabadi, Majaz Lakhnavi, and Faiz Ahmed Faiz. He liked Iqbal, even though he had reservations about the poet's highly conservative religious worldview. Sahir's writing style, some critics mention both as a compliment and criticism, is not much different from Faiz's. Sahir was introduced to socialist thinking by his friend Gopal Mittal. He adopted the communist perspective and even came to the conclusion that progressive writing was not possible without a strong belief in the communist ideology.[8] At the same time, it must be stated that Sahir never became a member of the Communist Party of India.

---

[7] Surinder Deol, *The Treasure: A Modern Rendition of Ghalib's Lyrical Love Poetry* (New Delhi: Partridge Publishing, 2018, 2nd ed.), 74.
[8] Balwant Singh, '*Ham Ke Thehre Ajnabi*', 48.

While commenting on Sahir's poetry, K.A. Abbas, the noted film director and writer, offered this opinion:

> Sahir is among the three great living poets. He demonstrates complete mastery over the art of poetic writing, and his use of metaphors and similes is complete and appropriate, which clearly falls outside the competence of many other poets. Even some older poets lack his sophistication as a poet.... One thing that separates Sahir from others is that in his writing there is lyricism coupled with a message of social awakening. He stands against communalism, and unlike some of his seniors, he does not sing about the bulbul's doings in the garden. He sings songs that are relevant today. He sings songs of the earth.[9]

Poet Ali Sardar Jafri supports the above assessment:

> Some people have tried to downgrade Sahir's poetry by calling him a poet of teenagers. But this insult in fact is a compliment. Ask yourself, how many poets are capable of writing poetry that would be loved by teenagers? Young people have fresh feelings and their emotions speak of their purity. They have dreams and resolutions of achieving something unique in life. The way Sahir captures these feelings, no contemporary poet is capable of doing that.[10]

Jafri quotes a couplet by the Iranian ghazal master Hafiz and he paraphrases its meaning: One morning a bulbul told a newly blossomed flower in the garden, 'Don't be too proud. Many flowers like you have blossomed in this garden and they have withered away.' The flower smiled and replied, 'Your blunt talk has hurt me. No lover has ever spoken to his beloved in this crude manner.' Sahir does not hold back anything. He speaks his mind.

[9] K.A. Abbas, 'Hamare Mulk Ke Maqbuul Tariin Shaa'yir', Fan aur Shakhsiyat, 17–18, 1985: 94–5.

[10] Ali Sardar Jafri, 'Sahir Ka Shaayiraana Mizaj', Fan aur Shakhsiyat, 17–18, 1985: 96.

Since Sahir was inspired by Faiz, some people make the mistake of believing that Sahir just copied Faiz. To this, Jafri responds:

> This misunderstanding arises from the fact that both these poets mix romance with social protest. But Faiz does not have the same concept of the beloved as Sahir. Makhdoom and Majaz also mix romance with protest. But these four poets have different temperaments. Sahir deploys a lover's arrogance, egotism, and self-indulgence that was last seen in Ghalib's poetry.[11]

Sahir was conscious of the fact that his was primarily a man's world where women had limited opportunities for progress. As women are forced by society to account for all their actions, this adversely affects man–woman relationships. Any healthy society would remove all barriers to equality among the sexes. There was the related issue of sexual exploitation, about which Sahir felt passionately, and two of his poems, 'Woman' and 'Whorehouses', deeply touched the conscience of the nation when Guru Dutt's film *Pyaasa* was released in 1957.

Sahir wrote long and short poems, *ghazal*s, and lyrics, but essentially, he was poet of the nazm. It was only through the medium of the nazm that he was able to convey his revolutionary message and romantic hues. Writing a ghazal was comparatively an easy task for him.

About This Book

This book attempts to present the genius of Sahir through his literary output, one that extends well beyond his work as a song writer. We start with events of Sahir's early life and take them up to the publication of *Talkhiyaan*, his first collection of poems, in the early 1940s, and its aftermath (Chapter 1). A remarkable feat of Sahir's genius was his long peace poem '*Parchhaaiyan*', published in 1955. Although this work is not that well known even among Sahir's fans, it is a testament to

---

[11] Jafri, '*Sahir Ka Shaa'yiraana Mizaj*', 98.

the fundamental longing of all humanity for peace and security. This poem was important at the time of its publication during the Cold War, and is still relevant today in the 21st century, when there are new and even more frightening threats to global peace. We cover this poem and its literary accomplishment in Chapter 2. Chapters 3 and 4 deal with Sahir's ghazals and *bhajans*. The epilogue concludes our journey with some closing thoughts and observations.

A few words about the translation. There are some unique challenges inherent in translating Urdu poetry into any of the international languages. Urdu poets use metaphors, similes, and phrases that lose their appeal when translated because they are like flowers of a tree that grows only in India and is watered and sustained by the air that we call Indian culture and history. This fragrance dies when transported to a different cultural milieu. The translator is therefore required to use his or her imagination and words and phrases in another language that give to the reader something close to the original flavour. Sahir has been poorly translated (this can be said of many other leading Urdu poets as well) and thus his work is hard to find outside the subcontinent. Pablo Neruda wrote in Spanish, but he is among the most loved poets in English. Rumi, because of the excellent translation by Coleman Barks, has found admirers across the world in the last two decades. This book is for the reader with little or minimal knowledge of Urdu or Hindi; I hope that they draw the same level of aesthetic satisfaction as the native reader.

There are three elements of my approach that I wish to highlight: I make use of simple, yet creatively vibrant language; I bring out the true meaning of what the poet wrote; and I endeavour to alluringly sculpt the finished product so that it looks and feels as good or as meaningful as the original. To what extent I have succeeded in this, you as a reader have the last word, and I would greatly appreciate your feedback.[12]

---

[12] I have translated all the works cited, except that of Akshay Manwani's, which is written in English.

1
Poems
Bitter and Sweet

This garden and this place
next to flowing Jamuna,
these sculpted doors and windows,
these arches and recesses.
An emperor
taking advantage of his wealth
has made fun of loves
and endearments of indigents like us.
My Beloved,
you should meet me
at some other place.

—'Taj Mahal'

When Sahir lived in Lahore before and, for a very brief period, soon after Partition, he became friends with several poets and writers who were either already famous or became famous in later years. This included Hameed Akhtar, Ibn-e-Insha, Qateel Shifai, Saadat Hasan Manto, Agha Shorish Kashmiri, Abdul Hamid Adam, and Ahmad Rahi. But the person who made the most difference in launching Sahir's literary career was Ahmad Nadeem Qasmi. A poet and a highly respected literary figure, it was he who wrote a preface for *Talkhiyaan* when the book was reprinted by a literary publishing house in 1944. This event can best be compared to an earthquake, the tremors of which were felt as far away as Bombay. Sahir, who had left his native town of Ludhiana filled with great anguish and disappointment and was simmering with the agony of failed love relationships, felt a wave of optimism suddenly run over every nerve of his body, and he captured his feelings in a short poem titled 'Yesterday and Today':

There was a drizzle yesterday.
Clouds, too, gathered yesterday.
And the poet thought about it.

These clouds, dreams of the sky,
are shadows of her tresses.
Riding shoulders of the wind,
tavern after tavern gathered in the sky.
Seasons will change, flowers will bloom,
flurries will rain honey.
In the bright greenery of the fields
colourful headscarves will be seen
flying in the air.
Shepherds will sow in the air
new songs harmonized on their flutes.
In the mango groves
strangers will open up their hearts.
Flickers of lightning will be seen
from the forehead of a maiden on a swing.
The still waters of the pond will reflect
multiple images of stars
that will be seen blinking their eyes.
They will come down in their intricate pathways
holding on to hems of colourful attires.
This earth, these flowers, this sky, these stars,
they will transform themselves into dreams.

There was a drizzle yesterday.
Clouds, too, gathered yesterday.
And the poet thought about it.

Kaifi Azmi saw a copy of *Talkhiyaan* when it was sent to him for review by the daily newspaper where he worked, and he was flabbergasted.

Who *was* this man? How is it that *he* had never heard anything about him before? This was the reaction of many other established poets and critics as well. Very soon, the booksellers were receiving requests: 'I want the book that has the poem '*Taj Mahal*'.' *Talkhiyaan* has the unique distinction of being the only Urdu book other than *Divan-e Ghalib* that has been published in dozens of editions in both Urdu and Hindi. Each time an edition appeared, Sahir made some additions and deletions, and this process continued until the early 1960s.

This chapter includes selections from *Talkhiyaan's* first and subsequent editions. As you read these poems, you will find three things that stand out. First, there is romance, a feeling of excitement and mystery associated with young love, often intermingled with tension that seeks an urgent resolution. Second, there is a deep connection with nature—physical beauty extending from celestial objects to hills and mountains, rivers and lakes, to evergreen fields and gardens filled with flowers. Third, there is a call for social justice and an end to all forms of oppression—for total revolution, either loud and clear, or in hushed tones, something that slithers under the surface. These are signature qualities of Sahir's poetry, which I call 'bittersweet'. I found them in *Talkhiyaan* and they were there in everything he wrote later in his life, including his film songs.

The period between 1950 and 1980, that is, when Sahir entered the film industry and when he passed away, was highly creative and rewarding for him, but from a literary standpoint some people find it disappointing. During these 30 years Sahir published only two literary books, *Parchhaaiyaan* and *Aao K Koi Khwaab Bunein*, excluding a collection of his film lyrics called *Gaata Jaye Banjaara*. Sahir argues with people who do not consider his film lyrics literary creations. This is what he had to say about literature as is commonly understood, and about film songs as a new form of literature.

Films are the most effective medium of our age. If they are used to bring about constructive and positive change, people's thought processes as well as social progress can be influenced greatly and very rapidly ... Because I have a connection with both films and literature, I find it necessary to point out a couple of things for the benefit of my literary friends. A film's songwriter does not have the freedom that a literary poet has. A songwriter has to always remain circumscribed by the film's plot. He has to choose his words and thoughts according to the description of each character in the film.… That is why it is important for a critic to look at a film's songs, and not only consider which poet has written the songs, but for which character the songs have been written … It is obvious that with all such preconditions, the output cannot be ignored, as it has its own significance. It has its own reach which is far greater than books, magazines, radio, and theatre, and through this we can have our views reach a greater number of people in lesser time. I have always striven to bring songwriting as close to literary poetry and to use it to provide new political and social perspectives to people.[1]

How do we judge the quality of a poem? Ali Sardar Jafri draws from one of the couplets written by Mirza Ghalib and gives it a little twist to highlight the qualities of a good poem. He writes:

A good poem should satisfy four requirements identified by Ghalib as icons of beauty—*saadgi* [simplicity], *purkaari* [skillfulness], *bekhudi* [intoxication], *hushiaari* [prudence or wisdom]. When these criteria are met, the poem becomes a complete paragon of beauty and it steals the heart of the reader.[2]

Sahir easily meets these requirements. There is simplicity in his tone that is hard to miss. This simplicity also turns into complexity when the poet tries to address major societal issues—and he does it with a great degree of finesse and skilfulness. Although most progressive poets stayed away from mysticism, Faiz revealed a mystic streak that actually made his revolutionary poetry so appealing. Sahir shares this trait with Faiz, and sometimes his words reach mystical heights, gaining readers' attention and winning their hearts. Lastly, Sahir shows his deep commitment and wisdom when it comes to issues of war and peace—the threat of another war between India and Pakistan in particular and the nuclear holocaust in general.

[1] Manwani, *Sahir Ludhianvi*, Ch. 14.
[2] Jafri, '*Sahir Ka Shaa'yiraana Mizaj*', 240.

4

When it comes to reading Sahir's nazms, we can follow either the chronological order in which the poems were written and notice how the poet's thinking evolved over time, or place them in clearly identifiable categories that are thematic and easy to grasp. The latter option, I feel, provides a better reading experience as the reader can find everything in one place, for instance, on love, nature, revolution, or social maladies like prostitution. Poems in this chapter can therefore grouped into categories. These divisions are not mutually exclusive and they overlap in many ways: love and longing; love and nature; inner journeys; oppressed masses and revolutionary change; exploitation of women; yesterday, today, tomorrow; the feudal order; the pathfinders.

Love and Longing

Sahir's romantic life started in the very first year of his college. There was a Hindu girl, the daughter of a local Congress Party leader, imbued with the same kind of nationalistic feelings as Sahir's, and who did not hide her romantic feelings for him. While he valued her affection and her respectful demeanour, he was not in love with her. Perhaps the only thing that he liked about her was her 'dark and deep eyes', which distinguished her from other girls. He expressed his feelings about her in the following couplet:

On the terrace of a house in front of me
is a girl waiting for someone.
We are not related, though when I look at her
a fire blazes in my being.

saamne ik makaan ki chhat par muntazir koi ek larki hai
mujh ko us se nahien ta'llaq kuchh phir bhi siine mein aag bharki hai

-
This affair unfortunately did not last very long; the girl fell ill and died shortly thereafter. This came as a great personal shock to Sahir. He had thought about many things but not about death. He went to the cremation grounds and saw the body of his lady love slowly being

consumed by the flames. Here are a few lines from a poem that Sahir wrote in his first love's memory:

The paradise of my longings
is now reduced to a handful of ashes.
The treasure of my love
is nothing more than these ashes.
These ashes belong to a virgin beauty.
These ashes are the cinders of the longings of my heart.
Of desires that arose, ashes of my lonely moments.
In these ashes I see the glitter of stars.
In these ashes is hidden an earthly, innocent houri.
Let the flames leap up once again
to finally end the regimen of my anguish.

ab meri aarzuuon ki jannat y raakh hai
sarmaaya-e hasuul-e mohabbat ki raakh hai
y meri shaa'yiri ki kahaani ki raakh hai
y raakh ek paak javaani ki raakh hai
y raakh mere dil ki tammanna ki raakh hai
zauq-e talab ki jurrat-e tanha ki raakh hai
is raakh mein falak ke sitaaron ka nuur hai
is raakh mein zamiin ki maa'suum huur hai
sho'le phir ek baar isi raakh se utha
aur khatam kar de mere masaa-ib ka silsila

He cried for days, even got one of her framed photos from a friend. Then, as it happens in such cases, time healed his heart and the girl eventually became a distant memory.

The second romance started a year or two later, this time with a Sikh girl[3] who lived in the college hostel located on the college premises.

---

[3] Some of Sahir's friends from his days in Ludhiana who have written about these romantic episodes have provided both correct and incorrect names of these girls. I think it is improper to reveal their identities since fate

She has been described by Sahir's friends as a 'delicate and elegant beauty', 'a girl with very sharp features', 'a girl like a moving portrait'. His own feelings are reflected in these lines:

In the midst of a shower of colours
I'm enjoying the company of sweet smells.
Who knows whether it is night or day!

rangon ki barkha hai khushbu ka saath hai
kis ko pata hai ab din hai k raat hai

As we can visualize, this must have put a lot of pressure on the girl, knowing that her Sikh parents would never allow her to marry a Muslim boy. The girl, who was known to be cheerful before this affair started, had nothing but sadness, tears rolling down her cheeks, once their love story became the talk of the college. Sahir's poem 'On Seeing Someone Heartbroken' reflects his state of mind:

I have nothing.
I can live by my tears.
But for God's sake,
don't live in the prison of your own sorrow.
No big deal
that the world snatched you away from me.
Who belongs to whom?
Think about it.
I swear in the name
of my despairing youth.
I am happy.
My love needs no bouquets.

I can erase
all joy left in my soul.

---

never gave these girls any opportunity to either admit to these affairs or to express their feelings about them.

But I cannot erase
your happiness.
I can hand myself over
to the grip of death
but I cannot bear the burden
of this adversity.
There are other sorrows
besides the sorrow
of my unrequited love.

mera to kuchh bhi nahien hai main to ro ke ji luunga
magar khuda ke liye tum asiir-e gham n raho
hua hi kya jo zamaane ne tum ko chhiin liya
yahaan p kaun hua hai kisi ka socho to
mujhe qasam hai meri dukh-bhari javaani ki
main khush huun meri mohabbat ke phuul thukra do

main apni ruuh ki har ik khushi mita luunga
magar tumhaari masarrat mita nahien sakta
main khud to maut ke haathon mein saunp sakta huun
magar y baar-e masaaib utha nahien sakta
tumhaare gham ke siva aur bhi to gham hain mujhe
najaat jin se main ik lahza pa nahien sakta

Since Sahir did not talk about this affair other than in his poetry,
our knowledge about it rests on the testimony of some of his close
friends. According to one such account, while the college was closed
for the summer vacations, Sahir asked the girl to come to meet him.
This news leaked and reached the college principal. Any contact
between male and female students outside college hours was against
the rules, and so the principal asked both of them to not show up
when the college reopened. There is another account that says that
the principal conveyed his unhappiness to Sahir and his beloved but
did not take any action. In any case, the girl left the college either
as a result of her own choice, or under pressure from her family.
It is said that Sahir was so upset that he travelled to the girl's village

and tried to contact her, but the girl refused to meet him, now fully aware that this relationship had reached a dead end. The story about Sahir's 'expulsion' from the college is quite famous. But those who have looked into this incident have found no evidence in the college records that proves that Sahir was expelled. It was Sahir who decided to leave the college and the city.

And so Sahir arrived in Lahore in 1941. He tried to restart his student career twice, once in Dayal Singh College and then in Islamia College, but he did not succeed in earning his bachelor's degree. But, as it happens, when one door closes another one opens. By this time he had written enough poems for a slim anthology, but no literary publisher was ready to bet on a young, unknown poet. It was Gurbaksh Singh, publisher of the Punjabi magazine *Preet Lari*, who agreed to publish the book in 1943 using cheap paper and binding. A better version of the book was published in 1944, and overnight Sahir found himself at the front line of progressive poets that included names like Faiz Ahmed Faiz, Ali Sardar Jafri, Majrooh, and Kaifi Azmi. Sahir was soon awarded editorship of a prestigious literary magazine called *Adab-e Latif*—a great achievement for a boy who had just turned 23.

Before we come to the poems in this section about love and longing, we have to visit one more romance that has become the hallmark of Sahir's public biography.

Preet Nagar is a small township midway between Amritsar and Lahore. It was the brainchild of Punjabi novelist and essayist Gurbaksh Singh, who had helped Sahir publish *Talkhiyaan*. Singh was a trained engineer and Marxist who established Preet Nagar as a commune following Marxist principles of shared living. This was the same man who published the popular monthly magazine *Preet Lari* in Punjabi and a few other languages, including Urdu. He had asked Sahir to edit the Urdu edition of his magazine.

Amrita Pritam, the young iconic beauty ('a chiselled piece of marble, like a goddess in a temple', as she was described by writer C.L. Kavish) and promising Punjabi poet attended a poetical symposium in Preet Nagar where Sahir was also present. Amrita may have read Sahir's poetry but this was the first time she saw him face-to-face. It was love at first sight, at least as far as she was concerned. 'After that there was a river of fire through which I floated day and night,' she wrote. This happened around 1944. She was married at that time and did not get a divorce until the early 1960s. This 'relationship' lasted several decades and Amrita wrote about it extensively in her autobiography, but Sahir never publicly commented on it. Therefore, whatever we know about this strange one-sided affair comes to us in Amrita's own voice:

> I remember once at some mushaira, people were taking Sahir's autographs. When everyone moved away and I was the only one standing in the line, I pushed my hand towards him and opened my palm. He scribbled his name on my palm. He said, 'I have signed a blank cheque. You can cash it any time you like.'[4]

Those who saw Amrita around that time said that she was a stunningly beautiful woman, a virtual heart-stopper. She also contained oceans of literary talent. When she pushed her arm towards Sahir, she was not looking for an autograph. She was virtually saying, 'Take me, take my hand, and I will come with you, leaving everything behind. I want you and just you….' Did Sahir get the message? If he didn't, it was strange. If he got it and then decided not to do anything about it, it was even stranger. What stopped him from reaching out? Was it lack of self-confidence? Or just lack of interest in a romantic relationship?

Amrita talked of three occasions when she experienced complete awakening as a woman, and one of those occasions was with Sahir. He was suffering from high fever and chest congestion, and breathing heavily. She took some Vicks and rubbed it around his throat and chest. While doing this, she had something akin to an out-of-body experience. She felt that if she could continue to do what she was doing for the rest of her life it would give her immense happiness. It was around this time that Sahir presented her a framed copy of 'Taj Mahal'.

[4] Amrita Pritam, 'Kore Kaghaz Ki Daastaan', Adab Saaz, 12–14, 2010: 50.

Amrita's obsession with Sahir took many forms. When she gave birth to her son, she used to see the outline of Sahir's face on her child's. She was not offended when she heard rumours that the child was Sahir's. When the boy was 13, even he asked his mother, 'Am I Sahir uncle's son?' To this her answer was an emphatic no. But the boy insisted, 'You can tell me the truth because I do like Sahir uncle.'

Amrita and Sahir met several times in Delhi and Bombay. In particular, she recalled a meeting she had with him when he was staying in a luxury hotel in New Delhi. She went to see him with Imroze, her live-in companion. Sahir took out three glasses and poured some whiskey. They sat for a long time, saying very little. No one drank anything. That evening, around 11 p.m., Sahir called Amrita and told her that he had emptied all the three glasses and written a ghazal. (This ghazal, 'Mere saathi khaali jam', would go on to become a famous film song).[5] Some people, while commenting on this meeting, have stated that Sahir was upset that Amrita came to see him along with her friend, but no one really knows what was on his mind.

Some of the conversations that took place between these two 'lovers' give the impression that Sahir was playing some kind of a mental game with her. Notice the following conversation:

Sahir: Why don't the two of us go and live in China?
Amrita: What will we do living in China?
Sahir: We shall write poetry.
Amrita: We can write poetry here without going to China.
Sahir: Yes, we can, but if we go to China we will never come back.[6]

When Amrita heard that Sahir had passed away, her mind went back several years to when both of them had attended the first Asian Writers' Conference held in Delhi in 1955:

All the writers attending the conference got their name badges. Sahir removed mine and stuck it on his coat. Then he removed his badge

---

[5] Amrita Pritam, 'Yaadon Ke Lams', Fan aur Shakhsiyat, 17–18, 1985: 88–93.
[6] Manwani, Sahir Ludhianvi, Ch. 7.

and attached it to my jacket. If someone noticed that we were wearing each other's badges, Sahir would say that the organizers must have made a mistake. But we did not consciously correct the mistake … It was actually my turn to die. The angel of death made a mistake. It just looked at my badge that Sahir was wearing![7]

Amrita wrote a poem in Punjabi about her feelings. Here is the English translation and Urdu transliteration. As you read the poem, you feel embankments are breaking open and you are suddenly drowned in the wild rush of failed longings.

I was on this side of the shore,
you were on the other side.
Strong bars of iron separated us.
I was on this side of the shore,
you were on the other side.
I did not try to remember you.
You had spoken softly:
I want these iron bars to stay as they are.
I want my gaze fixed on you.
Unable to touch you, or come closer
and this way, my love,
I want these moments
to pass away and die.
I was on this side of the shore,
you were on the other side.
Even today these shores separate us.
In the walls of life I see
these formidable iron bars.

Today, why do I find tears in my eyes?
Today, why do I find sighs on my lips?
Today, why do I find these wounds
on my forehead after I hit the walls?

---

[7] Pritam, '*Kore Kaghaz Ki Daastaan*', 50.

Today, why do I feel something burning in my heart?
Today, why do I find shakiness in my emotions?
Today, why do I feel the urge to break into pieces
these iron bars to get closer to you?
Today, why don't you say with a smile on your lips:
let these iron bars stay
but let my gaze stay fixed on your countenance,
I can't touch you, I can't come near you,
but my love, I want moments of this life
to pass away and die like this.

main is paar thi tu us paar
aur ham donon mein haail thein
lohe ki mazbuut salaakhein
main is paar thi tu us paar
aur phir tujh ko yaad nahien kya
tu ne aahista se kaha tha
yuunhi rahein y salaakhein
yuunhi nigaahein tujh p jami hon
chhu n sakuun paas aa n sakuun main
aur yuunhi meri maah paarah
ziist ke lamhe biite jaaein
main is paar thi tu us paar
aaj bhi pehle hi ki suurat
main is paar huun tu us paar
ziist ki diivaaron mein ab bhi
siina taane ustaadah hain
lohe ki mazbuut salaakhein

aaj hain kyon aankhon mein aansu
aaj labon par kyon hain aahein
diivaaron se sar takra kar
aaj hain kyon maathe p khraashein
aaj hai kyon siine mein jalan si
aaj hai kyon jazbaat mein halchal
aaj salaakhein tor ke yaksar

13

kyon hai mujhe paane ki tamanna
aaj bhi pehle hi ki suurat
hanste hanste kyon nahien kehta
yuunhi rahein daaim y salaakhein
yuunhi nigaahein tujh p jami hon
chhu n sakuun paas aa n sakuun main
aur yuunhi ... meri maah paarah
ziist ke lamhe biite jaaein[8]

This section on Love and Longing contains 13 poems that mirror different stages and states of a romantic relationship, from love at first sight to bidding goodbye.

An Encounter

This is a deeply romantic poem about a visit that called attention to some psychological issues. What happens when one person is tranquil and the other is nervous and restless? When people blame luck as the reason for their failure, are they not admitting that they didn't try hard enough or the right way? The poet does not say much in the end and leaves it to the reader to reflect on the situation.

When you were agitated
it didn't bother me much,
but seeing your tranquillity
I've become nervous and restless.
Knowing how much it might hurt you,
I lost myself today
in your thoughts and recollections.

Some people might be bothered
that you came to my home like this.
Like if you came another time

---

[8] Chander Varma and Salman Abid, *Main Sahir Huun* (Delhi: Takhleeqkar Publishers, 2014), 72–4.

you won't find my home.
I raised my eyes
with a lot of uncertainty
as if no one familiar
would have raised his eyes like this.

You smiled, but then
you suppressed your smile
thinking that the smile
would not get you in touch
with your pain.
You stopped as if your prayers
would not be answered
more creatively.
When you left
with your feet immersed in grief,
you simply said:
there is a journey
that you can't avoid
but getting a companion
for the journey
is a matter of luck.

When you were agitated
it didn't bother me much,
but seeing your tranquillity
I've become nervous and restless.
Knowing how much
it might hurt you,
I just engrossed myself
in your thoughts.

Ek Mulaqaat

teri tarap se n tarpa tha mera dil lekin
tere sukuun se bechain ho gaya huun main

y jaan kar tujhe kya jaane kitna gham pahunche
k aaj tere khayaalon mein kho gaya huun main

kisi ki ho ke tu is tarah mere ghar aayi
k jaise phir kabhi aaye to ghar mile n mile
nazar uthaayi magar aisi be-yaqiini se
k jis tarah koi pesh-e nazar mile n mile

tu muskuraayi magar muskara ke ruk si gaayi
k muskuraane se gham ki khabar mile n mile
ruki to aaise k jaise teri riyaazat ko
ab is samar se ziyaada samar mile n mile
gayi to sog mein duube qadam y kah ke gaaye
safar hai shart shariik-e safar mile n mile

teri tarap se n tarpa tha mera dil lekin
tere sukuun se bechain ho gaya huun main
y jaan kar tujhe kya jaane kitna gham pahunche
k aaj tere khayalon mein kho gaya huun main

On Seeing Someone Heartbroken

Sahir's college friends have mentioned that he wrote this poem for a fellow student at his college in Ludhiana, the one who was the reason he had to leave. The autobiographical part, real or imagined, makes the poem relevant for our study, but even if we forget this, the poem still stands on its own. It starts with deep empathy and compassion, and goes on to offer hope while taking responsibility for the ways in which the poet's behaviour might have enhanced his beloved's suffering. Towards the last part of the poem we see the twist for which Sahir is quite famous, namely, moving away from what is personal to what is collective, social, and political. This is a technique used by all progressive poets. Faiz is known to make masterful use of this. The poet starts with the strains of a broken love affair, then he comfortably takes the reader to scenes of poverty and hunger in the streets, the colourful lifestyles of the wealthy, images of war and destruction in distant lands. All this has nothing to do with his personal story, but in comparative terms, it is more significant than the plight of one person facing the sudden dissolution of his relationship. It is a powerful read from start to finish and is considered to be one of Sahir's best poems.

For many days now
I find you depressed and heartbroken.
I don't know what blows
you are actually nursing.
That naughtiness, that twinkle,
that laughter is no more.
You look at everything
with an unfulfilled desire.
You try to hide your restlessness
in your silence.
You have become a broadcaster
of your own secrets.

If my hope was dashed, so be it.
What is hope after all?
It is nothing but vacillation.
Don't worry about my life's sorrows.
The sorrow of life is nothing
but the sorrow of one's being.
Show some mercy to your beauty
and to your beautiful gait.
Fidelity is deceptive, long-lasting lust,
nothing more.

Why should I complain
about your indifference?
It is just a demand of my wrecking,
and my feelings.
I know you are scared
of the world around you.
I understand this world.

It is a strange world.
Here death thrives
under the veil of life.
The sound of a broken instrument
is the soul of a melody.

I suffer no grief
coming from your separation.
In the world of my imagination
you are always close to me.
You were right when you said,
'Do not come to see me.'
But please tell me
why are you depressed and heartbroken?
Don't take exception
to my speaking so openly.
You know that you are my life's aspiration.

I have nothing.
I can live by my tears.
But for God's sake,
don't live in the prison of your own sorrow.
No big deal
that the world snatched you away from me.
Who belongs to whom?
Think about it.
I swear in the name
of my despairing youth.
I am happy.
My love needs no bouquets.

I can erase
all joy left in my soul.
But I cannot erase
your happiness.
I can hand myself over

to the grip of death
but I cannot bear the burden
of this adversity.
There are other sorrows
besides the sorrow
of my unrequited love.
I cannot free myself
from them for a moment.

Under the portals of these tall houses
you hear the shouts of hungry beggars
every step of the way.
There is the tumult of poverty
and hunger in all homes.
Humanity mourns in all directions.
There is hustle-bustle in the factories
where they cast slabs of iron.
Buried underneath
is the soul song of countless people
who are destitute.

In the open streets,
there is the lustre of colourful saris.
Lying in the huts
are dead bodies without shrouds.
There is the din and rush of cars
in the main street.
Sitting on railroad tracks
are poor kids looking pale.

In street after street
are young faces sold.
Beautiful eyes covered
with a mist of melancholy.
There is war
and saucy young men of my land

whose youth is being auctioned.
There is the grasp and clutch of law and order
everywhere.
There is humiliation, slavery,
and helplessness.

These sorrows are enough
to finish off my life.
By being depressed and heartbroken,
please do not add to my misery.

Kisi Ko Udaas Dekh Kar

tumhein udaas si paata huun main kaii din se
n jaane kaun se sadme utha rahi ho tum
voh shokhiyaan voh tabassum voh qahqahe n rahe
har ek chiiz ko hasrat se dekhti ho tum
chhupa chhupa ke khamoshi mein apni bechaini
khud apne raaz ki tashhiir ban gaii ho tum

meri ummid agar mit gayi to mitne do
ummid kya hai bas ik pesh-o pas hai kuchh bhi nahien
meri hayaat ki ghamgiiniyon ka gham na karo
gham-e hayaat gham-e yak nafas hai kuchh bhi nahien
tum apne husn ki raa'naaiyon p rahm karo
vafa fareb hai tuul-e havas hai kuchh bhi nahien

mujhe tumhaare taghaaful se kyun shikaayat ho
meri fana mere ehsaas ka taqaaza hai
main jaanta huun k duniya ka khauf hai tum ko
mujhe khabar hai y duniya a'jiib duniya hai
yahaan hayaat ke parde mein maut palti hai
shikast-e saaz ki aavaaz ruuh-e naghma hai
mujhe tumhaari judaayi ka koi ranj nahien
mere khayaal ki duniya mein mere paas ho tum
y tum ne thiik kaha hai tumhein mila n karuun

magar mujhe y bata do k kyun udaas ho tum
khafa n hona meri jurrat-e takhaatub par
tumhein khabar hai meri zindagi ki aas ho tum

mera to kuchh bhi nahien hai main to ro ke ji luunga
magar khuda ke liye tum asiir-e gham n raho
hua hi kya jo zamaane ne tum ko chhiin liya
yahaan p kaun hua hai kisi ka socho to
mujhe qasam hai meri dukh-bhari javaani ki
main khush huun meri mohabbat ke phuul thukra do

main apni ruuh ki har ik khushi mita luunga
magar tumhaari masarrat mita nahien sakta
main khud to maut ke haathon mein saunp sakta huun
magar y baar-e masaaib utha nahien sakta
tumhaare gham ke siva aur bhi to gham hain mujhe
najaat jin se main ik lahza pa nahien sakta

y uunche uunche makaanon ki deorhiyon ke tale
har ek gaam p bhuuke bhikaariyon ki sada
har ek ghar mein y aflaas aur bhuuk ka shor
har ek samt y insaaniyat ki aah o buka
y kaar-khaanon mein lohe ka shor o ghul jis mein
hai dafn laakhon ghariibon ki ruuh ka naghma

y shaahraahon p rangiin saariyon ki jhalak
y jhonparon mein ghariibon ke bekafan laashe
y maal road p kaaron ki rel pel ka shor
y patriyoon p gharibon ke zard-ru bachche

gali gali mein y bikte hue javaan chehre
hasiin aankhon mein afsurdagi si chhaii hui
y jang aur y mere vatan ke shokh javaan
khariidi jaati hain uthti javaaniyaan jin ki
y baat baat p qaanuun o zaabte ki grift
y zillatein y ghulaami y daur-e majbuuri

21

y gham bahut hain meri zindagi mitaane ko
udaas rah kar mere dil ko aur ranj n do

Taj Mahal

This poem is a strong statement about wealth inequality, and the exploitation of the poor by the rich. It criticizes the general attitude that ignores these fundamental issues and chooses to dwell, instead, on something beautiful, becoming an escape for the masses from poverty-stricken lives in which there is no beauty, not even a concept of beauty.

Ali Sardar Jafri mentions an interesting fact—that Sahir had not seen the Taj before he wrote his poem. He might have written a different poem if he had. The Taj is not a miracle that Emperor Shah Jahan somehow brought into being. It is the magic of the artistry of Indian and Iranian craftsmen, designers, and builders. But poetry does not account for real occurrences. It rises higher and rides the waves of imagination, and that is where Sahir excels.

The Taj has an iconic presence across the world as an elegy to a lover. When poets wrote about the Taj Mahal, it was about its grandeur and beauty, and the love story it symbolized. For lovers, therefore, going to Taj Mahal was like a pilgrimage. Then came Sahir. It seems he picked up a big stone and shattered a myth that was deeply ingrained in the Indian consciousness. The Taj is no place for lovers. It is a symbol of one man's arrogance and his ability to exploit the labour of thousands of hapless workers. We remember Shah Jahan and Mumtaz Mahal, but who remembers those who suffered building this mausoleum? Sahir's poem was a mini earthquake. India's popular culture was badly shaken.

There were two kinds of reactions: Some were outraged that a young unknown poet had dared to cast doubt on the sanctity of a loving relationship between an emperor and his consort. But there were many more who were curious and wanted to know about the poet's point of view. This poem was the primary reason *Talkhiyaan* became a bestseller. As Gopi Chand Narang pointed out in the

Foreword to this book, both Faiz and Sahir entered the literary world with poems that touched the masses at the deepest level. In the case of Faiz, it was his poem '*Mujh Se Pehli Si Mohabbat Mere Mahbuub N Maang*', and for Sahir it was '*Taj Mahal*'.

The poem is crafted as a conversation between two lovers, with one of them believing that the Taj Mahal is a symbol of love, and the other holding a more revolutionary stance that it is a symbol of exploitation. That is why there is the suggestion: 'You should meet me at some other place.' There are a number of arguments that systematically smash folklore surrounding this monument. There is an undercurrent of socialist thinking (the rich exploit the poor for their own selfish ends) that you could expect from a progressive poet. But what impressed most readers was the sincerity and emotional detachment with which the poet builds his case. The poem, leaving everything aside, is a pleasure to read for its lyrical quality.

Taj is a symbol of love for you.
This valley of colours is something
that you cherish.
My Beloved, you should meet me
at some other place.

What is the point of the penniless
coming to this assembly of royals?
Inscribed on this path
are signs of royal majesties.
What is the meaning
of love-laden souls journeying here?

My Beloved,
behind the veils
of well-publicized constancy,
you should have seen
the marks of majestic power.
You who find
graves of dead royals comforting,

23

you should look back
at our own dark hearths.

Numerous people in this world
have fallen in love.
Who says that their emotions
were not sincere?
But there is nothing
that publicizes their stories,
because those people
were down and out like us.

This monument, these graves,
these enclosures, these castles,
these pillars of the greatness
of the ruling monarchs
are but a colourful mosaic
decorating the world,
in which is mixed the blood
of our ancestors.

My Beloved,
those people must have also fallen in love
whose artistry created this amazing beauty.
The graves of their loved ones
have no displays and no names.
No one has ever taken
a paper lantern to their graves.

This garden and this place
next to the flowing Jamuna,
these sculpted doors and windows,
these arches and recesses.
An emperor
taking advantage of his wealth
has made fun of the affections

and loves of indigents like us.

My Beloved,
you should meet me
at some other place.

Taj Mahal

taaj tere liye ek mazhar-e ulfat hi sahi
tujh ko is vaadi-e rangiin se a'qiidat hi sahi
meri mahbuub kahiin aur mila kar mujh se

bazm-e shaahi mein ghariibon ka guzar kya ma'ni
sabt jis raah mein hon satvat-e shaahi ke nishaan
us p ulfat bhari ruuhon ka safar kya ma'ni

meri mahbuub pas-e parda-e tashhiir-e vafa
tu ne satvat ke nishaanon ko to dekha hota
murda shaahon ke maqaabir se bahalne vaali
apne taarik makaanon ko to dekha hota

an-ginat logon ne duniya mein mohabbat ki hai
kaun kahta hai k saadiq n the jazbe un ke
lekin un ke liye tashhiir ka saamaan nahien
kyun k voh log bhi apni hi tarah muflis the

y imaarat o maqaabir y fasilein y hisaar
mutlaq-ul hukm shahanshaahon ki azmat ke satuun
daaman-e dahr p us rang ki gulkaari hai
jis mein shaamil tere aur mere ajdaad ka khuun

meri mahbuub unhein bhi to mohabbat ho gi
jin ki sannaa'ii ne bakhshii hai use shakl-e jamiil
un ke pyaaron ke maqaabir rahe benaam o numuud
aaj tak un p jalaayi n kisii ne qindiil

y chaman-zaar y jamuna ka kinaara y mahal

y munaqqash dar o diivaar y mahraab y taaq
ik shahanshaah ne daulat ka sahaara le kar
ham ghariibon ki mohabbat ka uraaya hai mazaaq

meri mahbuub kahiin aur mila kar mujh se

Sometimes

Imagine a colourful visual—iconic actor Amitabh Bachchan holding the charming Rakhi in his arms under a tree, while snow falls, a fire burns nearby, and a beautiful song plays in the background. That is how most people remember 'Kabhi Kabhi Mere Dil Mein Khayaal Aata Hai'. The poem so impressed film director Yash Chopra that he wanted to make a movie with this as its theme song. But the poem as written and published in Talkhiyaan contained difficult Urdu words that could not be easily grasped by the ordinary filmgoer. So Yash Chopra asked Sahir to rewrite the poem for his film. Both versions still retain great similarity, and judging by any standard, still make for a great love poem.

Sometimes this thought
crosses my mind—
if I were able to spend my life
in the shade
of your soft tresses,
it could have retained
its lushness and greenery.
This gloomy darkness
which is now
the fate of my life
could have opened itself
to the bright rays of your eyes.
It would not be surprising
If I gave up the world
and became engrossed
in your alluring loveliness.

Your delicate body
and your half-open eyes—
these are like exotic stories
in which I would have
immersed myself.

If the harsh realities of life
beckoned me
I would have gulped sweetness
from your lips.
Even if life wandered
howling, bare-headed
I would have hidden myself
and lived
in the dense shade of your locks.

But this did not happen
and now this is the situation:
I don't find you around.
There's not even the agony of your absence
or the longing to have you back.
My life is lived in such a way
that it does not look for any support.

I have embraced all the suffering
that life could offer.
I am treading
some unknown paths,
and dreadful shadows
are advancing in my direction.
In these frightful fields of spikes,
I'm caught between life and death.

There is no path,
no destination in sight,
and no clue where to find some light.

Sahir

My life is wandering
in zones of emptiness.
I might be lost
in this hollowness.
I know this,
but my dear soulmate,
I need not even say it.

Sometimes this thought
crosses my mind.

Kabhi Kabhi

kabhi kabhi mere dil mein khayaal aata hai
k zindagi teri zulfon ki narm chhanv mein
guzarne paati to shaadaab ho bhi sakti thi
y tiirgi meri ziist ka muqaddar hai
teri nazar ki shu'aaon mein kho bhi sakti thi

a'jab n tha k main begaana-e alam ho kar
tere jamaal ki raa'naaiyon mein kho rahta
tera gudaaz badan teri niim baaz aankhein
inhi hasin fasaanon mein mahv ho rahta

pukaartiin mujhe jab talkhiyaan zamaane ki
tere labon se halaavat ke ghuunt pi leta
hayaat chiikhti phirti barhana sar aur main
ghaneri zulfon ke saaye mein chhup ke ji leta

magar y ho n saka aur ab y aalam hai
k tu nahien tera gham teri justuju bhi nahien
guzar rahi hai kuchh is tarah zindagi jaise
use kisi ke sahaare ki aarzu bhi nahien

zamaane bhar ke dukhon ko laga chuka huun gale
guzar raha huun kuchh anjaani rahguzaaron se

muhiib saaye meri samt barhte aate hain
hayaat o maut ke purhaul khaarzaaron se

n koi jaadah-e manzil n raushni ka suraagh
bhatak rahi hai khalaaon mein zindagi meri
inhi khalaaon mein rah jaaunga kabhi kho kar
main jaanta huun meri ham nafas magar yuunhi
kabhi kabhi mere dil mein khayaal aata hai

A Poet of the Moment

'*Main Pal Do Pal Ka Shaa'yir Huun*' was another poem that was used for *Kabhi Kabhi*. It was written before the film was conceived, and has an autobiographical aura that is hard to miss.

I am a poet of the moment
and my story is as short as a moment.
Brief is my existence and my youth.

Many poets came before me;
they came and moved along.
Some shared their sighs,
some their melodies but
they all moved along.

They were a story of a moment.
I too am a story of the moment.
Tomorrow I will separate myself from you,
though today I am part of you.

If in these few moments
I am able to say something,
I would consider myself fortunate.
You listened to me in this moment
—that kindness means a lot to me.

Tomorrow there will be other poets
who can string tiny blossoms

to new melodies.
Their words will be better than mine;
their listeners will better than you.

Each generation is like a crop of the season,
it grows and then it is chopped.
Life is a precious thing that gets divided
into smaller and smaller units.

I am like the wave that rose high
but it is going to be absorbed back into the ocean.
I am like the dream of the soil
and I will go back to sleep in the soil.

Who will remember me in the days to come?
Why should anyone think of me?
People are busy doing things.
Why would they waste their time on me?

Main Pal Do Pal Ka Shaa'yir Huun

main pal do pal ka shaa'yir huun pal do pal meri kahani hai
pal do pal meri hasti hai pal do pal meri javaani hai
mujh se pehle kitne shaa'yir aaye aur aa kar chale gaye
kuchh aanhein bhar kar laut gaye kuchh naghme ga kar chale gaye
voh bhi ik pal ka qissa the main bhi ik pal ka qissa huun
kal tum se juda ho jaauun ga go aaj tumhaara hissa huun
pal do pal mein kuchh kah paaya itni hi saa'dat kaafi hai
pal do pal tum ne mujh ko suna itni hi inayaat kaafi hai
kal aur aayein ge naghmon ki khilti kaliyaan chun-ne vaale
mujh se behtar kahne vaale tum se behtar sun-ne vaale
har nasl ik fasl hai dharti ki aaj ugti hai kal kat-ti hai
jiivan vo mahngi mudra hai jo qatra qatra bat-ti hai
saagar se ubhri lahar huun main saagar mein phir kho jaauun ga
mitti ki ruuh ka sapna huun mitti mein phir so jaauunga
kal koi mujhe yaad kare kyun koi mujh ko yaad kare
masruuf zamaana mere liye kyun vaqt apna barbaad kare

Single-minded

It is an unwritten, centuries-old tradition of Urdu poetry that the lover treats the beloved with extreme gentleness, even reverence. Questioning the beloved and offering her stern advice is breaking with this tradition. Among the Urdu greats, only Ghalib has done so, and sparingly. Sahir joins Ghalib, but he goes a step farther. Instead of showering his beloved with compliments, the lover in 'Single-minded' questions her decision and issues her an ultimatum: stick with me if you have the guts—or settle down with someone of your parents' choosing. In Sahir's defence, we could say that this was his reaction to the messages he had heard from the people around him—you can do this but not that. Or he had heard a girlfriend tell him: 'I love you, but I can't do anything against the wishes of my parents.'

Why do you show me images of days gone by?
Why do you bother the one who has lost his way?
That beautiful promise which was not fulfilled—
why do you remind me of its meaning?
You should turn your life into a blazing flame.
Don't let yourself become a pile of silent ash.

I'm not convinced of any mystical happenings.
Don't lay flowers before my portrait
Who says sighs provide relief in times of distress?
Don't open yourself to ailments that you don't need.
With love in your heart for a rebellious soul
you are getting enmeshed in legal intricacies.
I understand sincerity is a trick of our civilization.
Why do you treat rituals as something to believe in?
If you worry about the world,
then don't shed tears thinking about me.
If you have the courage, pick up the flag of rebellion.
Otherwise, get married to whoever your parents
choose for you.

Yaksui

a'hd-e gum-gashta ki tasviir dikhaati kyun ho
ek aavaara-e manzil ko sataati kyun ho
voh hasiin a'hd jo sharminda-e iifa n hua
us hasein a'hd ka mafhuum jatati kyon ho
zindagi sho'ala-e bebaak bana lo apni
khud ko khaakistar-e khaamosh banaati kyun ho
main tasavvuf ke maraahil ka nahien huun qaail
meri tasviir p tum phuul charhaati kyun ho
kaun kahta hai k aahein hain masaaib ka ilaaj
jaan ko apni abas rog lagaati kyun ho
ek sarkash se mohabbat ki tamanna rakh kar
khud ko aaiin ke phandon mein phansaati kyun ho
main samajhta huun taqaddus ko tamaddun ka fareb
tum rusuumat ko iimaan banaati kyun ho
jab tumhein mujh se ziyaada hai zamaane ka khayaal
phir meri yaad mein yuun ashk bahaati kyun ho
tum mein himmat hai to duniya se baghaavat kar do
varna maan baap jahaan kahte hai shaadi kar lo

Masterpiece

This poem seems to be a continuation of the thought process we witnessed in the previous poem, 'Single-minded'. Love has reached a breaking point, principally because of the choices the beloved has made. There are a number of hints that she is ready to embrace a life of material comfort and has decided to give up on the lover who has neither fame nor wealth. The poet is trying hard to adjust to this new reality and he does this by virtually lampooning her. In the end, the poet takes this process to an extreme when he suggests to the painter to make some changes to her appearance in the portrait. The final insult comes in the last two lines:

> Here, where I stand,
> show a bright, shiny automobile.

It is a revenge poem—a genre nearly unknown in Urdu poetry.

Painter,
I have come to return
your masterpiece.
Add a tinge of saffron
to those radiant cheeks.

Infuse some courage
in these demure eyes.
Relax the wet creases
of her lips.

Let her heart's passion
become visible
in the colours of her forehead.

Add a bit of solemnity
to the smile on her face.
Diminish the conical heights
of her youthful bosom.

Chop the bulk of her dense hair
but make them more lustrous.
Take away the nobility in her eyes
and add some humility to her persona.

Yes, let her sit on a sofa
instead of a chair.

Here, where I stand,
show a bright, shiny automobile.

Shaahkaar

musavvir main tera shaahkaar vaapas karne aaya huun
ab in rangiin rukhsaaron mein thori zardiyaan bhar de

hijab-aaluud nazron mein zara bebaakiyaan bhar de
labon ki bhiigi bhiigi silvaton ko muzmahil kar de
numaayaan rang-e peshaani p aks-e soz-e dil kar de
tabassum aafriin chehre mein kuchh sanjiidagi bhar de
javaan siine ki makhruuti uthaanein sar-niguun kar de
ghane baalon ko kam kar de magar rakhshandgi de de
nazar se tamkanat le kar mazaaq-e aa'jizi de de
magar haan bench ke badle use sofe p bithla de

yahaan—meri baajaaye ik chamakati kaar dikhla de

A Poet's Worth

The poet talks about being forced to sell his love songs because of
economic hardship. There's a possibility that this was a lived experience
of Sahir's: in Lahore, he had no reliable source of income, and he lived
with equally indigent poets and writers. In the marketplace there is
a price for everything. But because art and poetry are subjectively
measured, artists and poets are generally not adequately rewarded. If
we see this poem as autobiographical, then it's ironical that the poet
who claimed injustice by the market system was hugely rewarded
by it in later years, and paid beyond his wildest imagination for his
love songs.

The songs
that your love inspired
me to write,
I have brought those songs
to the marketplace for sale.

Songs that were the foundation
of your love,
they would be auctioned
today.
Scales made of silver
will measure everything—

my thoughts, my poetry,
and my feelings.

Songs that were associated
with your being,
my poverty would make them look
like a thing for sale.
My needs for living
will eclipse
your beauty's splendour
and the stories we once shared.

In this age of capital
where labour has a price,
I can't keep my songs
just for my use alone.
Your charms, I know,
are owned by someone wealthy.
I have no right
even to the contours
of your memory.

I have brought those songs
to the marketplace for sale—
the songs
that your love inspired
me to write.

Fankaar

main ne jo giit tere pyaar ki khaatir likkhe
aaj un giiton ko baazaar mein le aaya huun
aaj dukaan p niilaam uthega un ka
tu ne jin giiton p rakhi thi mohabbat ki asaas
aj chaandi ke taraazu mein tulegi har chiiz
mere afkaar meri shaa'yiri mera ehsaas

Sahir

jo teri zaat se mansuub the un giiton ko
muflisi jins banaane p utar aayi hai
bhuuk tere rukh-e rangiin ke fasaanon ke e'vaz
chand ashiya-e zaruurat ki tamannayi hai

dekh is a'rsa-e gah-e mehnat o sarmaaya mein
mere naghme bhi mere paas nahien rah sakte
tere jalve kisi zardaar ki miiraas sahi
tere khaake bhi mere paas nahien rah sakte

aaj un giiton ko baazaar mein le aaya huun
main ne jo giit tere pyaar ki khatir likkhe

At the Crossroads

This poem reveals several layers of complexity and conflict. There is
a wall of wealth that divides the lovers. The lover has seen rejection
before, possibly because of his economic status. Now, the beloved
is making fresh overtures that make the lover cringe with doubt.
He can navigate all kinds of obstructions, but the wall of economic
inequality is insurmountable. The 'crossroads', therefore, is a mental
state. It does not offer a real choice. Love is a hapless victim of
society's preference for keeping social and economic boundaries
inviolate.

I shall not set foot
into those highrise mansions.
I had made this pledge once before.
In the face of the defeat
of my impoverished love,
my life showed itself
to be deficient and bewildered.
I had proclaimed
that in view of my ruination
I shall not sing
the melodies of love once again.
If someone called me

from behind the bamboo screen,
I shall not respond
but simply move ahead.
Even if a door opened,
I shall not return.

But then,
the fanciful smile
of your trembling lips
started to weave snares.
I could have taken a step back
but you were busy
choosing flowers for paths
I would tread.

Though my fanciful mind
made the snow fall,
a sudden nameless spark
struck my heart.
And when I saw your silent
and smouldering eyes,
my carelessly romantic mood
decided to return your love.

Please do not try to hide
the inducements of your eyes.
I can fathom the meaning
of this idiosyncrasy.
I can swear by the height
of the windows of your mansion
that I do understand
what I'm doing.

I shall not set foot
in those highrise mansions.

Sahir

I had pledged this once before.
On this crossroads
of capital and destitution,
life has experienced ignominy
and incertitude before.

Issi Doraahe Par

ab n un uunche makaanon mein qadam rakhuun ga
main ne ik baar y pahle bhi qasam khaayi thi
apni naadaar mohabbat ki shikaston ke tufail
zindagi pahle bhi sharmaayi thi jhunjhulaayi thi

aur y a'hd kiya tha k ba iin haal-e tabaah
ab kabhi pyaar bhare giit nahien gaauun ga
kisi chilman ne pukara bhi to barh jaauun ga
koi darvaaza khula bhi to palat aauun ga

phir tere kaanpte honton ki fusun kaar hansi
jaal bun-ne lagi bunti rahi bunti hi rahi
main khinchta tujh se magar tu meri raahon ke liye
phuul chunti rahi chunti rahi chunti hi rahi

barf barsaayi mere zehn o tasavvur ne magar
dil mein ik sho'la-e be naam sa lahra hi gaya
teri chup chaap nigaahon ko sulagte pa kar
meri bezaar tabi'at ko bhi pyaar aa hi gaya

apni badli hui nazron ke taqaze n chhupa
main is andaaz ka mafhuum samajh sakta huun
tere zarkaar darichon ki bulandi ki qasam
apne iqdaam ka maqsuum samajh sakta huun

ab n un uunche makaanon mein qadam rakhuun ga
main ne ik baar y pahle bhi qasam khaayi thi
apni naadaar mohabbat ki shikaston ke tufail
zindagi pahle bhi sharmaayi thi jhunjhulaayi thi

A Portrait in Colour

This poem is not very different from 'Masterpiece' and 'Single-minded'.
The poet as a defeated lover is in a sour mood. He is not shy of sharing
some harsh truths with his beloved. He calls her a 'distressed butterfly',
'an oppressive calamity'. She is someone whose delicate feet carry the
'weight of gold and silver'. She made a choice, and apparently gold and
silver won. But the lover is in no mood to forgive. He speaks his mind
and his words carry a bitter sting.

When I first saw you,
you looked like the dream of youth—
an immortal song of beauty,
a restless emotion of ecstatic love.

O distressed butterfly
of cheerful youth!
I didn't know
that you were a fragrance of captivity.
In your splendour
I saw shades of spring,
but I didn't know
you were an oppressive calamity.

Your delicate feet
carrying the weight of gold and silver
would never allow you to fly freely.
The sorrows you nursed
in search of comfort
would not allow your soul
to flourish.

In order to thrive
in the shade of wealth,
you sold the blood
of your heart and your love.

Taking advantage
of the riches
of mournful days,
you sold the pleasure
of impudent nights.

The flights of your imagination
show their wounds.
In your songs
the sorrows of your soul
are seen multiplying.
In your kohl-filled eyes
one sees the flames
of unfulfilled desires,
just like candles fluttering
in deserted,
final resting places.

What is the use
if under the colourful clothes,
the soul continues to burn,
shrivel, and dissolve?
There is a smile on the lips
just for show,
but life carries the burden
of sorrows and anguish.

A relaxed heart
is an argument
for the serenity of life,
but life simply
is not a basin for gold and silver.
It's a mixture of feelings,
desires, and afflictions—
it's not simply a story

about the arrangement
of your senses.

Instead of living like a worm
throughout your life,
it is better to have a moment
that makes your soul swell—
a moment that adds splendour
to your songs,
a moment that fills
your voice
with ecstasy.

Ek Tasviir-e Rang

main ne jis vaqt tujhe pahle pahal dekha tha
tu javaani ka koi khwaab nazar aayi thi
husn ka naghma-e javed hui thi ma'luum
i'shq ka jazba-e betaab nazar aayi thi

ai tarab zaar javaani ki pareshaan titli
tu bhi ik buu-e giraftaar hai ma'luum n tha
tere jalvon mein bahaarein nazar aati thiin mujhe
tu sitam khurda-e idbaar hai ma'luum n tha

tere naazuk se paron par y zar o siim ka bojh
teri parvaaz ko aazaad n hone dega
tu ne raahat ki tamanna mein jo gham paala hai
voh teri ruuh ko aabaad n hone dega

tu ne sarmaaye ki chhaanv mein panapne ke liye
apne dil apni mohabbat ka lahu becha hai
din ki taziin-e fasurda ka asaasa le kar
shokh raaton ki masarrat ka lahu becha hai

zakhm khurda hain takhayyul ki uranein teri
tere giton mein tiri ruuh ke gham palte hain

surmagiin aankhon mein yuun hasratein lau deti hain
jaise viraan mazaaron p diye jalte hain

is se kya faa'iida rangiin libadon ke tale
ruuh jalti rahe ghulti rahe pazhmurda rahe
hont hanste hon dikhaave ke tabassum ke liye
dil gham-e ziist se bhojal rahe aazurda rahe

dil ki taskiin bhi hai aasaish-e hasti ki daliil
zindagi sirf zar o siim ka paimaana nahien
ziist ehsaas bhi hai shauq bhi hai dard bhi hai
sirf anfaas ki tartiib ka afsaana nahien

umar bhar rengte rahne se kahin behtar hai
ek lamha jo teri ruuh mein vusat bhar de
ek lamha jo tere giit ko shokhi de de
ek lamha jo teri lai mein masarrat bhar de

A Beautiful Turn

This poem became a scene in the 1963 movie *Gumraah* and a beautiful song: 'Chalo Ik Baar Phir Se Ajnabi Ban Jaayein Ham Dono'. There are rumours and guesses about why Sahir wrote this poem and for whom, and where it was read for the first time. But they are irrelevant to our purpose. There are many good poems about creating a new relationship, but it is hard to find a satisfactory poem about the parting of ways. The lover is not preparing to kill himself. On the other hand, he has his emotions under control. He is thinking and speaking logically. The transition to becoming 'strangers' from lovers is a difficult one, but this poem clearly shows a path.

Let us once again
become strangers—the two of us.

Neither should I nourish
the hope that you would please my heart,

nor should you give me looks
that induce wrong impressions.
Neither do I want my heart's desire
revealed in my conversation,
nor should you give away any inkling
of the secrets of your inner struggle.

There is a hurdle that stops you
from moving forward.
People also tell me
that these allurements
do not belong to me anymore.
Walking alongside are defeats of my past.
You too have the company of shadows
of nights long gone.

* If a friendship turns sour
it is better to forget it.
If a relationship becomes a burden,
it is better to break it.
To a story that can't be brought
to its logical end,
it is better to give it a beautiful turn
before leaving it.

Let us once again
become strangers—the two of us.

Ek Khuubsurat Mo-r

chalo ik baar phir se ajnabi ban jaaein ham dono

n main tum se koi ummid rakhuun dil navaazi ki
n tum meri taraf dekho ghalat andaaz nazron se
n mere dil ki dharkan larkharaaye meri baaton se
n zaahir ho tumhaari kashmakash ka raaz nazron se

tumhein bhi koi uljhan rokti hai pesh qadmi se
mujhe bhi log kahte hain ki y jalve paraaye hain
mere hamraah bhi rusvaaiyaan hain mere maazi ki
tumhaare saath bhi guzri hui raaton ke saaye hain

taa'ruf rog ho jaae to us ka bhuulna behtar
ta'lluq bojh ban jaaye to us ko torna achcha
vo afsana jise anjaam tak laana n ho mumkin
use ik khuubsurat mo-r de kar chhorna achcha
chalo ik baar phir se ajnabi ban jaaen ham dono

Me or the Other

This is a love poem that Sahir probably wrote in his younger years. The person referred to in the poem is not addressed by name. It could be a real person or just an image from his dreams. The poet is struggling with the same dilemma that we have seen in several of his other love poems, namely, whether his love is strong enough to overcome the economic or class barriers. He brings sincere love to the relationship, but not bars of gold and silver. Will the beloved be satisfied with that? The poet waits for the answer.

The one who embellishes
the windows of my dreams,
I am asking you:
Do I pass through your dreams,
any time?
Ask your eyes and then let me know.
In the fate of my nights,
is there scope of a dawn?

Our four-day-old friendship
is not true friendship.
But it is becoming a torment
for the rest of my life.
It was already a bundle

of complications,
but now each breath
is becoming a huge burden.

My sleeping chambers
are just a wreckage of my lost sleep,
but you appear there
like an image seen in a dream.
At times belonging to me,
then like another.
At times the icon of affection,
then totally unconcerned.

I don't control my emotions
and my love for you.
You tell me
whether I should fall in love with you.
The desires that you have unleashed
with your smile,
should I give them an outlet?

You are the tiny blossom
of someone else's garden,
but my nights are always filled
with your fragrance.
You might be in any place
but I can swear by your flower-like cheeks,
your eyelashes follow
the direction of my eyes.

The warmth of your hands,
the sweet smell of your breath—
I find them submersed
in the fabric of my feelings.
The arms of my imagination
move around in search of you

in the smouldering loneliness
of cold nights.

Your generous demeanour
is real but even this reality
could prove to be a fabrication
of my own mind.
This heedful message
of your unpretentious eyes
could be an excuse
to do away with my heart.

I don't know
how my today will unfold
into my tomorrow.
Intimacy beyond a point
becomes the cause of penitence.
Colourful eyes
that circle the edges of my heart
could turn into an unknown other
in the wink of an eye.

Please interpret for me
the fatigued dreams
of my desires
associated with my distressed youth.
In the hem of your scarf
there are gardens
as well as deserted places.
What do I deserve?
What is my fate?
Better let me know.

Mata-e Ghair

mere khwaabon ke jhronkon ko sajaane vaali
tere khwaabon mein kahiin mera guzar hai k nahien

puuchh kar apni nigaahon se bata de mujh ko
meri raaton ke muqaddar mein sahar hai k nahien

chaar din ki y rifaaqat jo rifaaqat bhi nahien
u'mr bhar ke liye aazaar hui jaati hai
zindagi yuun to hamesha se pareshaan si thi
ab to har saans giraan-baar hui jaati hai

meri ujri hui niindon ke shabistaanon mein
tu kisi khwaab ke paikar ki tarah aayi hai
kabhi apni si kabhi ghair nazar aayi hai
kabhi ikhlaas ki muurat kabhi harjaayi hai

pyaar par bas to nahien hai mera lekin phir bhi
tu bata de k tujhe pyaar karuun ya n karuun
tu ne khud apne tabassum se jagaaya hai jinhein
un tamannaon ka izhaar karuun ya na karuun

tu kisi aur ke daaman ki kali hai lekin
meri raatein teri khushbu se basi rahti hain
tu kahiin bhi ho tere phuul se aariz ki qasam
teri palkein meri aankhon p jhuki rahti hain

tere haathon ki hararat teri saanson ki mahak
tairti rahti hai ehsaas ki pahnaayi mein
dhuundhti rahti hain takhayyul ki baanhein tujh ko
sard raaton ki sulagti hui tanhaayi mein

tera andaaz-e karam ek haqiiqat hai magar
y haqiiqat bhi haqiiqat mein fasaana hi n ho
teri maanuus nigaahon ka y mohtaat paayam
dil ke khuun karne ka ek aur bahaana hi n ho

kaun jaane mere imroz ka farda kya hai
qurbatein barh ke pashemaan bhi ho jaati hain
dil ke daaman se lipat-ti hui rangiin nazrein
dekhte dekhte anjaan bhi ho jaati hain

meri darmaandah javaani ki tamannaon ke
muzmahil khwaab ki taabiir bata de mujh ko
tere daaman mein gulistaan bhi hain viiraane bhi
mera haasil — meri taqdiir bata de mujh ko

Your Voice

It was Ali Sardar Jafri who once said that Sahir reminded him of Pablo Neruda (1904–1973), the Chilean poet who was hailed by Colombian Nobel laureate and novelist Gabriel Garcia Márquez as 'the greatest poet of the 20th century in any language'. For the sake of this comparison, it is important to point out that Neruda was a Left-wing intellectual, a member of the Chilean Communist Party, and a great admirer of the Soviet Union. Besides the ideology, what Neruda and Sahir share is their revolutionary zeal coupled with a big dose of passionate romance. Anyone who is familiar with Neruda's love poetry will hear his stylistic romantic murmuring in this poem.

There are all kinds of guesses about the subject of this poem. Irrespective of this speculation, it is one of Sahir's finest creations. Reading this poem, one draws the same satisfaction as from a romantic sonnet of Pablo Neruda. In the opening lines, the poet creates an atmosphere of calm expectation with help from stars that are pinching his eyes. But the silence and poise of the moment is shattered by the voice, like 'water rupturing the heart of a mountain to become a fountain'. The rest of the poem unfolds like a dream that comes back to life. Nothing happens. Expectation turns into disappointing wait and frustration. But there is a payoff. Good poetry brings us in touch with our feelings in the moment. There is no greater magic than the beloved's breath touching the lover's body. This is a poem that slowly enters our body. First we see it and read it. Then we hear its music in our ears, and then, it goes deeper and deeper until it plunges into our soul.

A desolate night and
the sighs of the surroundings
were heavily burdened.
There were nameless silhouettes

of grief hovering over my soul.
My heart was insistent
that you should come
to give me some comfort.
I was trying to put
my hapless heart to sleep.

For a long time,
the glitter of the stars
pinched my eyes.
For a long time,
my mind kindled
in this loneliness,
opening itself for questioning
by a former friend.
You did not show up
to be woven into the night.

All of a sudden,
I heard your voice,
pouring in from somewhere.
Like water rupturing
the heart of a mountain
to become a fountain.
Or, accidentally,
for the love of the land,
with great agitation
of mind and body,
a bright star
falling from the sky.

In the bitterness of the lonely night
there was a mixing of honey.
Colour spread around
in the darkness of the chambers.
For a long time,

I heard echoes
of your intoxicating voice,
like flowers suddenly blooming
in deserted places.

You are far away,
sitting in some voguish assembly.
Even then I feel that you have come
hiding my lost dreams
in the bundle of melodies,
bringing back my lost sleep.

On the surface of the night
the marks of your countenance.
The same old silent eyes
and the effortless way of seeing.
Descending headscarf
and the same elegant style of walking.
The same old amenable
and delicate persona.

You were not with me,
yet until the morning arrived
every breath that you took
touched my body
before it disappeared.
The act of seeing you
was like dew dripping
one droplet at a time.
Each moment that passed
was refreshed
by your fragrance.

If this is what you want
my soul of tranquillity,
I shall not look for your path

in the darkness of the night.
My tired eyes will find you
in the midst of rainy clouds
of song and verse.

If your love bothers me,
then my life will cast itself
in your carousing voice.
And this soul
that patiently yearns for you
shall become a song
restlessly moving on your lips.

Your melodies shall borrow
the coolness of your beauty
and find a place
in my slowly burning surroundings.
Whether I live for a few moments
or for a long time,
your songs will slowly put
my constantly awake night to sleep.

Teri Aavaaz

raat sunsaan thi bhojal thiin faza ki saansein
ruuh par chhaaye the be-naam ghamon ke saaye
dil ko y zid thi k tu aaye tasalli dene
meri koshish thi k kambakht ko niind aa jaaye

der tak aankhon mein chubhti rahi taaron ki chamak
der tak zehn sulagata raha tanhaayi mein
apne thukraaye hue dost ki pursish ke liye
to na aayi magar us raat ki pahnaayi mein

yuun achaanak teri aavaaz kahiin se aayi
jaise parbat ka jigar chiir ke jharna phuute

Sahir

ya zamiinon ki mohabbat mein tarap kar naagaah
aasmanon se koi shokh sitaara tuute

shahd sa ghul gaya talkhaaba-e tanhaayi mein
raŋg sa phail gaya dil ke siyaah-khaane mein
der tak yuun teri mastaana sadaayein guunjiin
jis tarah phuul chatakne lagein viirane mein

tu bahut duur kisi anjuman-e naaz mein thi
phir bhi mahsuus kiya main ne k tu aayi hai
aur naghmon mein chhupa kar mere khoye hue khwaab
meri ruuthi hui miindon ko mana laayi hai

raat ki sat-h par ubhre tere chehre ke nuquush
vohi chup-chaap si aankhein vohi saada si nazar
vohi dhalka hua aanchal vohi raftaar ka kham
vohi rah rah ke lachakta hua naazuk paikar

tu mere paas na thi phir bhi sahar hone tak
tera har saans mere jism ko chhu kar guzra
qatra qatra tere diidaar ki shabnam tapki
lamha lamha teri khushbuu se mo'attar guzra

ab yahi hai tujhe manzuur to ai jaan-e qaraar
main teri raah n dekhuunga siyaah raaton mein
dhundh leingi meri tarsi hui nazrein tujh ko
naghma o sh'er ki umdi hui barsaaton mein

ab tera pyaar sataaye ga to meri hasti
teri masti bhari aavaaz mein dhal jaaye gi
aur y ruuh jo tere liye bechain si hai
giit ban kar tere honton p machal jaaye gi

tere naghmaat tere husn ki dhandak le kar
mere tapte hue maahaul mein aa jaaein ge
chand ghariyon ke liye ho k hamesha ke liye
meri jaagi hui raaton ko sula jaaein ge

Love and Nature

Sahir's language has the uncanny ability to weave a harmonious interconnection between people and nature in a manner that is nothing short of miraculous. Nature in his poetry is not only scenic beauty; it is living and breathing presence. Every tree, every shrub, each blade of grass appears in a mystical state while making a rhythmic connection with the people around. Lovers not only find solitude; they find a home—a home that recognizes their presence and gives them the comfort and security they need.

Reaction

Talkhiyaan opens with a short poem that is enchantingly poignant. With great beauty—and brevity—the poem communicates the short-lived joy that a meeting with the beloved brings, for it is always tainted by the lengthy separation that follows, much like the day giving way to the night. It is lovers' fate to suffer in love—a perennial theme in Urdu love poetry.

After collecting
a few buds of cheerfulness,
I am lost in grief for a very long time.
Meeting you is a source of great joy,
but upon meeting you
I am overwhelmed with sadness.

Radd-e Amal

chand kaliyaan nashaat ki chun kar
muddaton mahv-e yaas rahta huun
tera milna khushi ki baat sahi
tujh se mil kar udaas rahta huun

A View

Poets who write about nature are generally those who have had personal experience of living in places where there are hills, valleys, rivers, forests, etc. Sahir was born in the flatland of Punjab and did not visit a hilly place until he was a successful film poet. Therefore, it was natural that when he picked up his pen to write a nature poem he described the beauty as seen by anyone in the rural Punjab. Notice references in the following poem to open spaces, pathways, fog, foliage, the chirpings of birds, and the sound of a Persian wheel. But no nature poem of his is complete without a subtle hint of romance. Notice the ingenious hint he drops in the last few lines of the poem.

Rays stealthily peeked
through the window
of the horizon.
Spaces opened up
in sheer indulgence and
pathways revealed their joyfulness.
The soft layer of fog
that had fallen
started to dwindle.
The young foliage lifted veils
that had covered its visage.
The fields were startled
by the chirpings of birds.
The Persian wheel started to sing
in mysterious tones.
The beautiful dew-laden pathways
started to embrace
shadows of the green trees.
At a distant mound
there was a flicker
of a hem of a veil.
In imagination,
millions of lamps
twinkled and shimmered.

Ek Manzar

ufaq ke dariiche se kirnon ne jhaanka
faza tan gaayi raaste muskaraaye

simatne lagi narm kohre ki chaadar
javaan shaakhsaaron ne ghonghat uthaaye
parindon ki aavaaz se khet chaunke
pur asraar lae mein reht gunganaaye
hasein shabnam aaluuda pagdandiyon se
lipatne lage sabz peron ke saaye
vuh duur ek tiiley p aanchal sa jhalka
tassavur mein laakhon diye jhilmilaaye

Shadows, Sunset, and the Mountain Trees

Sahir's love affair with nature is vividly presented in this beautiful ghazal. It begins with a panoramic view that shows us mountains and forests: the day is ending, and the last rays of the sun give us a view of purplish darkness as day meets and merges with the night. A blissful moment in the lap of nature and in the company of the beloved is nothing short of a miracle. This is the moment when humans embrace eternity.

Shadows of the fading evening
lurk on top of the mountain trees.
There is a grey light
mixed with purplish darkness.

Two time zones are meeting
in the form of two human hearts.
The delightful sky
has spread a basket full of colour.

In the still waters
are trilling melodies.
In the wet breeze
fragrances have settled their tents.

Why don't we engross ourselves
in this beautiful view?
There are swarms of light
and an abundance of delight.

Parbaton Ke Peron Par

parbaton ke peron par shaam ka basera hai
surmaayi ujaala hai champaayi andhera hai
dono vaqt milte hain do dilon ki suurat se
aasmaan ne khush ho kar rang sa bakhera hai
thahre thahre paani mein giit sarsaraate hain
bhiige bhiige jhonkon mein khushbuuon ka dera hai
kyon n jazb ho jaayein is hasiin nazzaare mein
roushni ka jhurmut hai mastiyon ka ghera hai

The Wait

When Sahir describes natural beauty, he paints a beautiful picture with his words. As the reader goes through the poem, he or she sees an image that unfolds itself. First you see the moon, then the clouds, the valleys, the springs. Each word adds to the picture, and each detail sharpens the painting. And yet, this is not just a description of nature; what makes the poem stand out is the poet's brilliance in fusing romance with nature. What good is natural beauty if the one you love is not standing beside you and enjoying the same scenery?

The moon is at peace with itself.
Resting in the bosom of sleep
the whole world is silent.

At some distance in the valley
milky clouds
are bending backwards
to kiss the mountain.

While nursing a multitude
of failed desires,
I am still waiting for you.

Come to the shadows
of these springs.

Who knows how long
the vivacity of my love
will last!

I can't say how long
life will show kindness
towards unfortunate ones
like myself!

I don't want to lose
the stars,
as it happens each day,
in the dust of the morning.

I want my eyes
to fall asleep
just for one night—
eyes that haven't seen
much sleep
because they are always
seeking you.

The moon is at peace with itself.
Resting in the bosom of sleep
the whole world is silent.

Intizaar

chaand maddham hai aasmaan chup hai
niind ki god mein jahaan chup hai

duur vaadi mein duudhiya baadal
jhuk ke parbat ko pyaar karte hain
dil mein naakaam hasratein le kar
ham tera intizaar karte hain
in bahaaron ke saaye mein aa ja

phir mohabbat javaan rahe na rahe
zindagi tere na muraadon par
kal talak mehrbaan rahe na rahe
roz ki tarah aaj bhi taare
sub-h ki gard mein n kho jaaein
aa tere gham mein jaagti aankhein
kam se kam ek raat so jaaein

chaand maddham hai aasmaan chup hai
niind ki god mein jahaan chup hai

Inner Journeys

Sahir gave very few interviews in which he talked about his personal life. The two exceptions were the ones he gave to poet Naresh Kumar Shad and novelist Balwant Singh.[9] When Shad asked him about his motivation for writing poetry, Sahir replied, 'Sometime[s] there are situations in one's personal and social life that can't be analyzed without the help of some form of poetical outlook. You need a special time for this. It is a state of mind that is not tolerant of any outside interference.' He also confirmed that he needed few meditative moments to write a poem or a lyric. Sahir was an introvert who cultivated the habit of going deep within himself for self-reflection. There are clearly a number of poems that he wrote (which are included in this section) that are the result of those inner journeys. He told Balwant Singh that there was a time when poetry came to him while he loitered at night on the streets in Ludhiana. 'But now I need quiet time without any interruptions,' he added.

An Incident

Poems that describe an event are easy to write but they can also fail to make an impact because everything that happens may not

---

[9] Naresh Kumar Shad, '*Sahir Ke Saath Ek Shaam*', *Fan aur Shaksiyat*, 17–18, 1985: 52–7.

be significant in the larger scheme of things. The title of this poem
gives the impression that the poet is reacting to something that just
happened. But that is not the case. This is not even a poem about an
incident; it is actually about a part of it, a departure. The poet is leaving
his past behind and responding to the call of the future. He may not
actually be sitting in his car and driving away; for all we know, it
could be the train that Sahir took from Ludhiana to go to Lahore. The
past has brought a lot of despair, but the poet is determined to leave
everything behind and move on.

In the cloister of the dark night
I hear the footsteps
of the coming daybreak,
in the midst of wet breeze

and lightly spreading mist.
Sitting alone in my car
I'm journeying
while my eyes

are bereft of sleep.
They are filled
with the veneer of dreams—
yearnings of the days past

and forgotten.
The future
with its moving hands
is calling me

even as I remember
events that have already
passed.
Joys that were lost

appear in my eyes,
swaying like tears

falling on my cheeks.
In the hollow spaces

of my chest,
is a shooting pain
that is spreading.
My failed longings are crying

but Hope tells me,
'Everything will be fine.'
The paths
that I have traversed

to reach here
are mapped
in my mind.
I wonder with what hopes

have I reached this place
and how much despair
I have brought with me.
How much despair!

Ek Vaaq'iya

andhyaari raat ke aangan mein y sub-h ke qadmon ki aahat
y bhiigi bhiigi sard hava y halki halki dhundhlaahat
gaari mein huun tanha mahv-e safar aur niind nahien hai aankhon mein
bhuule bisre armaanon ke khwabon ki zamiin hai aankhon mein
agle din haath hilaate hain pichhli biiti yaadein aati hain
gum gashta khushiyaan aankhon mein aansu ban kar lahraati hain
siine ke viiraan goshon mein ik tiis si karvat leti hai
naakaam umangein roti hain ummid sahaare deti hai
vo raahein zehn mein ghuumti hain jin raahon se aaj aaya huun
kitni ummid se pahuncha tha kitni maayuusi laaya huun

A *Melody of the Helpless*

This poem shows a strong inward focus. This is a 'confession' poem in which the lover shows his inability to do certain things. For a change, the beloved is faultless—the poet is not playing a blame game with her. Instead, he lists things that are desirable in a loving relationship, things that he cannot do. The admission of defeat that comes at the end is not uncommon in Urdu poetry.

You have met me in person
and in my thinking many a time.
Didn't you notice that I couldn't smile?
Despair is now a part of my being.
Even if I force myself,
melody is lost on my lips.
What did you see in me
that you fell in love with me?
I am unable to do any good to myself.
Soul nourishing are melodies
of the madness of love,
but I can't sing these sung songs.
I have seen
how the melodious instrument of love
breaks down.
I cannot raise my lute
to play a note.
My heart knows
the intensity of your feelings,
but I cannot release myself
from the grip of my own thoughts.
You will find yourself alone
even if I embrace you.
Even after surrendering myself to you
I shall not become a part of you.
I've sung love songs

with the sincerity of my heart,
but now I can't,
not even as a total hypocrite.
How can I make you a partner in life?
I'm unable to carry the burden
of my own being.

Let me drown myself
in the shallows of darkness.
Sorry, I'm unable to brighten up
the candle of desire.

Ma'zuri

khalvat o jalvat mein tum mujh se mili ho baar-ha
tum ne kya dekha nahien main muskara sakta nahien
main k maayuusi meri fitrat mein daakhil ho chuki
jabr bhi khud par karuun to gun guna sakta nahien
mujh mein kya dekha k tum ulfat ka dam bharne lagiin
main to khud apne bhi koi kaam aa sakta nahien
ruuh-afza hain junuun-e i'shq ke naghme magar
ab main in gaaye hue giiton ko ga sakta nahien
main ne dekha hai shikast-e saaz-e ulfat ka samaan
ab kisi tahriik par barbat utha sakta nahien
dil tumhaari shiddat-e ehsaas se vaaqif to hai
apne ehsaasaat se daaman chhura sakta nahien
tum meri ho kar bhi begaana hi paaogi mujhe
main tumhaara ho ke bhi tum mein sama sakta nahien
gaaye hain main ne khuluus-e dil se bhi ulfat ke giit
ab riyakaari se bhi chaahuun to ga sakta nahien
kis tarah tum ko bana luun main shariik-e zindagi
main to apni zindagi ka baar utha sakta nahien
yaas ki taariikiyon mein duub jaane do mujhe
ab main sham'a-e aarzu ki lau barha sakta nahien

Vanquished

The apathy and hopelessness in the previous poem intensifies in this one. It is a deeply depressing poem. It gives the impression of a conversation with the self that slowly turns into a conversation with the beloved. The poet confesses that he has brought unhappiness to his own life. He acknowledges that the beloved is reaching out to save him 'to reignite doused candles'. But it seems that it is too late. A frozen sadness surrounds his life. His soul has lost hope and passion. Although the promise of a new chapter of love in his life is alluring, that is not what the poet desires. The poem fulfils the promise conveyed by its title.

Embracing close to my heart
the dead body of hope,
I have brought unhappiness
to my life for long periods of time.
You made me face calamity a few times,
but I have done the job
of destroying my heart every day.
Whenever I saw silken dresses in my paths,
I remembered you in the midst of cold sighs.

And now in the filaments of my soul,
is a cloud of barrenness and downheartedness,
I find you coming towards me
bringing the dazzling rays of your cheeks,
and you are ready to reignite doused candles.

My beloved, this tumult of renewing constancy
does not suit my miserable youth.
The flowers that I selected for your footsteps—
I don't even have a hazy impression of them.

A frozen sadness engulfs my life.
My soul has neither hope nor passion.

The tumult of my yearnings and
of my distressed youth is now encumbered
by heavy chains.

In this desert, there is nothing except whirlwinds.
What do I have to gain
from the shadows of evasive rain clouds?
The lotus flowers of love in my heart
have lost their freshness.

What do I have to gain
from your regretful beauty?

These decayed silvery tears on your cheeks
are not the cure for my sorrows and griefs.
The message of your lovely eyes
to restart our affair
could be a regretful reversal;
but that is not what I desire now.

Shikast

apne siine se lagaaye huye ummid ki laash
muddaton ziist ko naashaad kiya hai main ne
tu ne to ek hi sadme se kiya tha do-chaar
dil ko har tarah se barbaad kiya hai main ne
jab bhi raahon mein nazar aaye hariiri malbuus
sard aahon mein tujhe yaad kiya hai main ne

aur ab jab k meri ruuh ki pahnaayi mein
ek sunsaan si maghmuum ghata chhaayi hai
tu ne damakte hue aariz ki shu'aayein le kar
gul-shuda sham'ayein jalane ko chali aayi hai

meri mahbuub y hangaama-e tajdid-e vafa
meri afsurda javaani ke liye raas nahien

main ne jo phuul chune the tere qadmon ke liye
un ka dhundla sa tasavvur bhi mere paas nahien

ek yakh-basta udaasi hai dil o jaan p muhiit
ab meri ruuh mein baaqi hai n ummid n josh
rah gaya dab ke giraan-bar salaasil ke tale
meri darmaanda javaani ki umangon ka kharosh

reg zaaron mein baguulon ke siva kuchh bhi nahien
saaya-e abr-e gurezaan se mujhe kya lena
bhujh chuke hain mere siine mein mohabbat ke kanval
ab tere husn-e pashimaan se mujhe kya lena

tere aariz p y dhalke hue siimiin aansu
meri afsurdagi-e gham ka mudaava to nahien
teri mahbuub nagaahon ka payaam-e tajdiid
ik talaafi hi sahi—meri tamanna to nahien

Failure

As the title suggests, the poem is an acknowledgement of personal collapse and foundering. There is a failure in love that sorrow could not cure. There were worldly challenges that were too difficult to respond to. The poet is caught up in a cycle that leads from one catastrophe to another, from one debacle to another. The damage is complete. Even the imagination is broken and scattered. There are soulless dilemmas that offer no escape routes. The poem suggests sadness and hopelessness that is more than a literary device. It is symptomatic of a real-life failure—perhaps a time when the poet moved from Ludhiana to Lahore. The dream of an academic degree up in flames and a personal love story wounded as if by thorns in a desert.

I tried for a time
to let go the sorrow of love.
I wanted to mix it
with the despair of endearment
and worldly troubles.

The same stories were moving
in my direction—until now.
The same flames
were hidden in my chest—until now.
The same useless wounds
were fresh in my chest—until now.
The same pointless desires
were youthfully alive—until now.
The same tresses
were unfurled over my nights.
The same eyes—until now—were
looking toward me.
The excess of sorrow
was unable to cure my grief.
My troubled thoughts
found no comfort.
My heart embraced
all kinds of worldly pain
but my fatigued soul
failed to learn a new style of frenzy.

My imagination is broken
and scattered like before.
The state of my dying feelings
is the same as before.
The same lifeless intents,
the same faded questions.
The same soulless dilemmas,
the same uneasy thoughts.

Ah, I want an end to this dissension
that goes from morn to eve.
I am a failure
and my effort to do anything good
is also a failure.

Naakaami

main ne har chand gham-e i'shq ko khona chaaha
gham-e ulfat gham-e duniya mein samona chaaha
vohi afsaane meri samt ravaan hain ab tak
vohi sho'ale mere siine mein javaan hain ab tak
vohi be-suud khalish hai mere siine mein hanuuz
vohi bekaar tamannayein javaan hain ab tak
vohi gesu meri raaton p hain bikhre bikhre
vohi aankhein meri jaanib nigraan hain ab tak
kasrat-e gham bhi mere gham ka mudaava n hui
mere bechain khayaalon ko sukuun mil n saka
dil ne duniya ke har ik dard ko apna to liya
muzmahil ruuh ko andaaz-e junuun mil n saka

meri takhayyul ka shiiraaza-e barham hai vohi
mere bujhte hue ehsaas ka aalam hai vohi
vohi-bejaan iraade vohi berang savaal
vohi beruuh kashakash vohi bechain khayaal

aah is kashmakash-e sub-h o masa ka anjaam
main bhi naakaam meri sa'ii a'mal bhi naakaam

A Conversation with Saaqi[10]

This is a ghazal which is being treated as a poem because of its thematic
novelty. A ghazal consists of a number of couplets, and each couplet
presents a thought or an idea that is complete in itself. But since this
ghazal has been written like a conversation, there is some consistency
in the flow of thoughts. At the outset, the poet attacks 'belief systems
and religion that make the human mind a bag full of unfounded stories
and myths'. People fail to understand reality because their minds are
polluted by a fog of false ideas. Old people are good at philosophizing,
while young ones can't separate good from bad. In this atmosphere

---

[10] Here, saaqi takes the role of alter ego—a person's alternative personality.

of not knowing what is real or unreal, love is lost. Poets sing songs of wine and honey while millions continue to starve and die. In the last couplet, Sahir indirectly points to a controversy that goes to the very heart of the progressive movement. The ghazal has a long history in Urdu literature, but for centuries, the themes that were embraced by the ghazal poets had to do with a make-believe world of love and beauty, of the songs of nightingales, wine flowing in taverns, and the allurements of the *saaqi*, the wine server. The fight for India's independence gained momentum in the 1920s, and the Progressive Writers' Movement formally came into being in the early 1930s; there was a demand, voiced among others by Ali Sardar Jafri, that the time had come to renounce Urdu's fascination with ghazals, and that progressive poets in particular should focus on the toils of farmers and labourers and prepare them for the coming 'red dawn'. But this idea gathered no steam because even progressive poets loved writing ghazals. Poets like Faiz refused to abide by any such directive. They continued to write ghazals because of its irrefutable—irresistible—charm, for the poet and the audiences.

Beliefs are hunches
and religion is the work
of our fanciful imagination.
From the start,
the human mind is a bag
full of unfounded stories
and myths.

Knowing reality,
to tell you the truth,
is like losing one's way.
The path of enlightenment
is purposefully wrapped
in ambiguity.

Old age honours
the ability to philosophize

what is considered
to be rational.
Youth is indifferent
to the consequences of its actions—
good or bad.

Desire is held a prisoner
of righteousness and rectitude.
Love is lost and is asking
for recognition of its identity.

My heart misses a beat
when I think of the perplexities
of my journey.
My desire to seek pleasure
and joy shames me
with its crudeness.

I have been sent to a place
where I have to rip up
the veil of the night—
a place where every morning
has a reflection of the night
on its edges.

In my hands
there is a cup of wine
and in yours there is a harp.
In our land
there is hunger,
there is lamentation,
there is moaning.

The time we live in
is a visage of frightening and
fast-approaching flames,
but on your lips, O Saaqi,

there is still the melody
of Khayyam.[11]

Khayaal-e Khaam

a'qaaed vahm hain mazhab khayaal-e khaam hai saaqi
azal se zehn-e insaan basta-e auhaam hai saaqi
'haqiiqat aashnaai' asl mein gum karda raahi hai
uruus-e aagahi parvarda-e ibhaam hai saaqi
mubarak ho za'iifi ko khirad ki falsafa raani
javaani be niyaaz-e ibrat-e anjaam hai saaqi
havas hogi asiir-e halqa-e nek o bad-e aa'lam
mohabbat maavara-e fikr-e nang o naam hai saaqi
abhi tak raaste ke pech o kham se dil dharakta hai
mera zauq-e talab shaayad abhi tak khaam hai saaqi
vahan bheja gaya huun chaak karne parda-e shab ko
jahan har sub-h ke daaman p aks-e shaam hai saaqi
mere saaghar mein mai hai aur tere haathon mein barbat hai
vatan ki sar-zamiin mein bhuuk se kohraam hai saaqi
zamaana barsar-e paikaar hai pur-haul sho'lon se
tere lab par abhi tak naghma-e khayyaam hai saaqi

Running Away

This is an escape poem—an escape from personal failings and conflicts
through a focus on what is hurting the poor, the masses. Compared
with what is going on in the world, one person's crazy passion becomes
insignificant. 'How long can I escape from the harsh realities of life?
How long can I sing sad songs while hiding from others?' These are
jarring questions. In reality, there is no place one can run to. The real
battle is where one stands. There is a very thin boundary between the
personal and impersonal. One person's pain cannot be separated from
the pain of all. Everything faces defeat in the end—whether it is love
or beauty. The poet's song drowns in a sea of despair.

---

[11] This is a reference to the Persian poet Omar Khayyam (1048–1131).

My crazy passion
to be constant in love
is on a downward path.
Your enchanting beauty
could not save you
from certain defeat.
Those longings
are now gathering
the dust of hopelessness.
Those things
that were nurtured
in the very act of your smiling,
the colourful magic
of the deceptions of your passion
has come to an end.
The reality,
when it faced calamity,
got badly burnt.
It's curtains now
for carefree dreaming.
My head and my heart
are really victims
of my savageness.
Those stars that sparkled
the shine of love—
those stars disappeared,
taking with them
the colours of beauty.
Your eyes had put to sleep
those pains,
but they came back
just as if they were stretching
their arms.
There is a strange feel of melancholy
in the face of brightness.
My eyes

are not asking for anything,
and my heart is not seeking
anything.
Your eyes, your hair,
your forehead, your lips—
my melancholy-prone temperament
doesn't want any of this.
I have run away
from the day-to-day struggles of life.
Your enchanting beauty
is hiding me from myself.
But the real world
pursues me here too.
Even here
I could not get
the paradise of stoicism.
I took a thousand mirrors
in each of my two hands
but life still crept
out from behind the closed drapes.
A thundering noise arose
around me and in that noise
were the musical arrangements
of my contentment.
How long can I escape
the harsh realities of life?
How long can I sing sad songs
while hiding from others?
Look at the mansion
where the shrill cry of a girl
who was rented for the evening
just hit its walls.
Look once again
at society's moralists
who just punished

two lovers with a sentence
of life in isolation.
Once again
in a dimly lit, poorly built shack,
the widow looked at her sobbing child
and her eyes were filled with tears.
Lo, once again someone's young daughter
was sold.
Once again,
the pride of someone's youth
was brought down.
Once again,
a gathering of farmers
faced machine guns
and they were fired upon
by those who claimed prior rights.
From the stillness of the prison
rose a piercing cry
and I remembered
the friends I have lost in this battle.
No, don't look at me
with your appealing glances.
My crazy passion
to be constant in love
is on a downward path.
Your enchanting beauty
could not save you
from certain defeat.

Gurez

mera januun-e vafa hai zavaal aamaada
shikast ho gaya tera fusuun-e zebaayi
un aarzuuon p chhaayi hai gard-e maayuusi
jinhon ne tere tabassum mein parvarish paayi

fareb-e shauq ke rangiin tilism tuut gaye
haqiiqaton ne havaadis se phir jila paayi
sukuun o khwab ke parde sarakte jaate hain
dimaagh o dil mein hain vahshat ki kaar farmaayi
vo taare jin mein mohabbat ka nuur taabaan tha
vo taare duub gaye le ke rang o ra'anaayi
sula gayi thiin jinhein teri multafit nazrein
vo dard jaag uthe phir se le ke angdaayi
ajiib aa'lam-e afsurdagi hai ruu b farogh
n ab nazar ko taqaaza n dil tamannaayi
teri nazar tere gesu teri jabiin tere lab
meri udaas tabii'at hai sab se uktayii
main zindagi ke haqaaiq se bhaag aaya tha
k mujh ko khud mein chhupaa le teri fusuun zaayi
magar yahaan bhi taa'qub kiya haqaaiq ne
yahaan bhi mil n saki jannat-e shakebaayi
har ek haath mein le kar hazaar aaiine
hayaat band darichon se bhi guzar aayi
mere har ek taraf ek shor guunj utha
aur us mein duub gayi ishraton ki shahnaayi
kahan talak koi zinda haqiiqton se bache
kahan talak kare chhup-chhup ke naghma pairaayi
vo dekh saamne ke pur shikoh aivaan se
kisi kiraaye ki ladki ki chiikh takraayi
voh phir samaj ne do pyaar karne vaalon ko
saza ke taur par bakhshi taviil tanhaayi
phir ek tiira o taariik jhonpari ke tale
sisaskte bachche p beva ki aankh bhar aayi
voh phir biki kisi majbuur ki javaan beti
voh phir jhuka kisi dar par ghuruur-e barnaayi
voh phir kisaanon ke majme p gun mashiinon se
huquuq yaafta tabqe ne aag barsaayi
sukuut-e halqa-e zindaan se ek guunj uthi
aur is ke saath mere saathiyon ki yaad aayi
nahien nahien mujhe yuun multafit nazar se n dekh

nahien nahien mujhe ab taab-e naghma pairaayi
mera junuun-e vafa hai zavaal aamada
shikast ho gaya tera fusuun-e zebaayi

Escape

This poem of deep self-reflection brings the past into focus once again. The poet feels revulsion and shame. There were many failures, including a love affair that got nowhere. When you are stuck, life offers few avenues to get away.

I am hounded
by visions of my past.
Those yesterdays
evoke nothing but revulsion.
The pointless desires
continue to shame me.
I regret having hopes
that were not fruitful.

Let my past stay buried
in the darkness.
My past is nothing
but a signpost of my shame.
My aspirations are realized
by the effort I put in.
It is nothing
but having a nameless distress.

I took the help
of many futile daydreams.
I adorned my chambers
to welcome someone.
I assembled obscure tracings
of several unsteady hopes

and settled them
in my dreams for someone.

Don't repeat to me
stories of my love affair.
Let me say
that I never wanted anything.
Those bacchanalian eyes
that have forgotten me.
I never said anything good
about those drunken blues.

Let me say
that I can live on my own
as of now.
My love crumbled
but my life is stable.
To embrace something
and to make her my own—
the desire was bad
but the way it sadly ended
is not.

The same locks of hair,
the same eyes, cheeks or body—
if I want them
I can get them anywhere.
Those lotuses
that were meant to blossom for her,
they can blossom somewhere else
away from her eyes.

Faraar

apne maazi ke tasavvar se hiraasaan huun main
apne guzre hue ayyaam se nafrat hai mujhe

apni be-kaar tamannaaon p sharminda huun
apni be-suud ummiidon p nadaamat hai mujhe

mere maazi ko andhere mein daba rehne do
mera maazi miri zillat ke siva kuchh bhi nahien
meri ummidon ka haasil meri kaavish ka sila
ek be-naam aziyat ke siva kuchh bhi nahien

kitni be-kaar ummidon ka sahaara le kar
main ne aivaan sajaaye the kisi ki khaatir
kitni be-rabt tamannaaon ke mub-ham khaake
apne khwaabon mein basaaye the kisi ki khatir

mujh se ab meri mohabbat ke fasaane n kaho
mujh ko kahne do k main ne unhein chaaha hi nahien
aur voh mast nigaahein jo mujhe bhuul gayein
main ne un mast nigaahon ko saraaha hi nahien

mujh ko kahne do k main aaj bhi ji sakta huun
i'shq naakaam sahi zindagi naakaam nahien
un ko apnaane ki khwaahish unhein paane ki talab
shauq bekaar sahi sa'i-e gham-e anjaam nahien

vohi gesu vohi nazrein vohi aa'riz vohi jism
main jo chaahuun to mujhe aur bhi mil sakte hain
voh kanval jin ko kabhi un ke liye khilna tha
un ki nazron se bahut duur bhi khil sakte hain

I'm Afraid

This beautiful love poem has a tension and tentativeness that reveals
the poet's uncertainty: Is it true, or am I dreaming? Sahir shines when
he is holding the banner of revolution, but he is equally at home
writing a love poem, and this one is a joy to read.

A tiny dash of smile
on your lips

rises in my imagination
time and again.
Suddenly, I think
about your cheeks,
like the flare of a candle
rages in the darkness.

The enchanting redolence
of your colourful apparel
turns itself into a dream
and dances in my mind.
With each bit of gentle breeze
in the cold silence of the night
I feel the warmth
of your breath and your body.

I can reveal the secrets
that are still smouldering
but I'm afraid of the attention
they would bring.
I can narrate the dreams
of the night
in the light of the day—
but I'm afraid
how those dreams
could be explained.

The weariness of your breaths
and the stillness of your eyes
in disguise could be
some kind of colourful naughtiness.
What I thought
was an expression of love—
that smile, that eloquence
could just be a habit of yours.

I'm thinking,
while I have come to meet you,
to analyse my thoughts
before I say anything.
I'm a stranger
and an outsider in your city.
I should understand
the meaning of your concerns
before I say anything.

I'm afraid
I might lose control of my feet
and I might not get the brace
of your ivory-coloured arms.
I might cry
in the silence of the black nights
and I might not get the edge
of your scarf.

Hiraas

tere honton p tabassum ki voh halki si lakiir
mere takhayyul mein rah rah ke jhalak ut-thi hai
yuun achaanak tere aa'riz ka khayaal aata hai
jaise zulmat mein koi sham'a bharak ut-thi hai

mere pairaahan-e rangiin ki junuun khez mahak
khwaab ban ban ke mere zehn mein lahraati hai
raat ki sard khamoshi mein har ik jhonke se
tere anfaas tere jism ki aanch aati hai

main sulagate hue raazon ko ayaan to kar duun
lekin un raazon ki tashhiir se ji darta hai
raat ke khwaab ujaale mein bayaan to kar duun
un hasiin khwaabon ki taabiir se ji darta hai

teri saanson ki thakan teri nigaahon ka sukuut
dar haqiiqat koi rangiin sharaarat hi n ho
main jise pyaar ka andaaz samajh baitha huun
vo tabassum voh takallum teri aa'dat hi n ho
sochta huun k tujhe mil ke main jis soch mein huun
pahle us soch ka maqsuum samajh luun to kahuun
main tere shahr mein anjaan huun pardesi huun
tere altaaf ka mafhuum samajh luun to kahuun

kahiin aisa n ho paanv mere tharra jaayein
aur teri marmarien baanhon ka sahaara n mile
ashk bahte rahein khaamosh siyaah raaton mein
aur tere reshmi aanchal ka kinaara n mile

Before Killing Oneself

Why do people decide to kill themselves? What is the state of mind of a one who is weighing death as an alternative to life? Sahir gives a glimpse into the despair that may prompt one to consider suicide. As a romantic poet, he offers a situation: that of failure in love, which triggers the frustrated lover to contemplate suicide. Is that a sufficient reason? If we look deeper, however, the poem reveals a layer that comes across as an elucidation of what death or dying is really about. The last stanza of the poem smoothly transforms itself into a meditation about life and death. It reminds us of Pablo Neruda's poem 'Nothing but Death' ('*Solo la Muerte*') in which he talks about death coming to the person who is dying. Neruda writes: 'Death arrives among all the sound/like a shoe with no foot in it, like a suit with no man in it,/ comes and knocks, using a ring with no stone in it, with no finger in it,/comes and shouts with no mouth, with no tongue, with no throat./ Nevertheless its steps can be heard/and its clothing makes a hushed sound, like a tree.'[12]

[12] Edward Hirsch, *How to Read a Poem* (New York: Harcourt, 1999), 36–8, translation by Robert Bly.

In Sahir's poem death does not arrive, does not make any sound, and is not seen; it is just a cave or a series of caves. The person who is dying descends into a cave with a candle in his or her hand. Why a candle? Metaphorically, it could mean that a lover's death is no different from that of a moth. Therefore, the candle's flame is the ground where a lover's life, like that of a moth, separates itself from the body. By holding a candle, the person contemplating suicide controls the space where death occurs. This definitely disempowers the angel of death. Or it could mean that the person who is dying is not ready to descend into the darkness of the cave of death without seeing or knowing what they are getting into and that is why there is entry into the cave while the candle is lighted. This is the symbolic power for the one who is taking his or her life to 'cross the never ending frontier of death'.

Dear me,
this cruel darkness,
these wafts of breeze—
who knows
whether there would be dawn
after this night.
Let me look
at your window once more.
My eyes are losing sight;
they might not see anything
soon.

There is still some light
in your warm sleeping chambers.
Blue curtains
still allow some light
to filter through.
Locked in a stranger's arms
you might still be swaying
your fragrant tresses.

In the company of the candle
that is slowly dying
invisible shadows are advancing
with open hands.
Who can wipe the smouldering tears
off my eyes?
Who can untangle the knots
of messy hair?

Alas, these caves of death
and the prison of a candle.
I have spent all my life
in these dark homes.
Life seems to be a crime,
the work of insensitive nature.
It was a real thing
but it was spent
in a few short snippets.

How many comforts
made fun of me
in the palaces?
How many closed doors had
my youth to encounter?
How many hands have
knitted smooth, glossy fabric?
But the fate of my garments
was covered by patches.

Enduring agony and torture
in this slaughterhouse of people,
how can one amuse oneself
with the images of a better tomorrow?
If you have crawled all your life,
your life is your punishment.

If it were a torment of a day or two
one could bear it.

The same darkness still envelopes
the surrounding domains.
Who knows
when it would end—
the distillation of man's blood.
Who knows
when the youth of darkly dressed ambience
would refresh itself.
Who knows
when the fate of oppressed folk
would reverse itself.

There is still some light
in your warm sleeping chambers.
Today, I would descend
into the caves of death.
And alongside a candle
that is losing its breath
I will pass through
the never-ending
frontier of death.

Khudkushi Se Pahle

uff y bedard siyaahi y hava ke jhonke
kis ko ma'luum hai is shab ki sahar ho k n ho
ik nazar tere dariiche ki taraf dekh to luun
duubti aankhon mein phir taab-e nazar ho k n ho

abhi raushan hain tere garm shabistaan ke diye
niil-guun pardon se chhanti hain shua'aen ab tak
ajnabi baanhon ke halqe mein lachakti hon gi
tere mahke hue baalon ki radaaein ab tak

Sahir

sard hoti hui batti ke dhuen ke hamraah
haath phailaaye badhe aate hain bojhal saaye
kaun paunchhe meri aankhon ke sulaghte aansu
kaun uljhe hue baalon ki gir-h suljhaaye

aah y ghaar-e halaakat y diye ka mahbas
u'mr apni inhi taariik makaanon mein kati
zindagi fitrat-e behis ki puraani taqsiir
ik haqiiqat thi magar chand fasaanon mein kati

kitni asaayishein hansti rahiin aivaanon mein
kitne dar meri javaani p sada band rahe
kitne haathon ne buna atlas o kamkhwaab magar
mere malbuus ki taqdiir mein paivand rahe

zulm sahte hue insaanon ke is maqtal mein
koi farda ke tasavvur se kahaan tak bahle
u'mr bhar rengte rahne ki saza hai jiina
ek do din ki aziyyat ho to koi sah le

vohi zulmat hai fazaaon p abhi tak taari
jaane kab khatm ho insaan ke lahu ki taqtiir
jaane kab nikhre siyah posh faza ka jauban
jaane kab jaage sitam khurda bashar ki taqdiir

abhi raushan hain tere garm shabistaan ke diye
aaj main maut ke gharon mein utar jaauun ga
aur dam torti batti ke dhuen ke hamraah
sarhd-e marg-e musalsal se guzar jaauunga

Madam

This poem was triggered by a casual remark by Amrita Pritam about the shabbiness of Sahir's friends in Lahore, in the way they looked and dressed, and the way they addressed each other. Although Sahir was born to a land-owning family, he was raised by a single mother who faced severe financial problems. In view of this, Sahir perceived himself as a product of the struggling lower middle class, people living on the borderline of poverty, though they nursed ambitions to be artists or poets. On the other hand, Amrita Pritam was married to a businessman and in her social circles one's appearance mattered, as did grooming and social graces. It is clear from the poem that Sahir was upset by this opinion of his friends by someone who was privileged: she belonged to the upper middle class, and was steeped in the values taught by Western education. As a progressive and someone who shared the Marxist view of the world, Sahir goes straight to the Marxist idea of dialectical materialism—social class determines and shapes one's consciousness. Poetry thus turns into a diatribe. A casual and friendly remark ignites a mini class warfare.

Why are you upset without any reason, Madam?
If people say it, they must be right.
My friends may not have learnt the civilized ways.
Humans may not be residing in my part of the world.

Civilization draws its strength from the light of the capital.
Where we are, civilized ways can't prosper.
Poverty can't remove the longing for pleasure.
Hunger can't be cast into a gentlemanly mould.

No surprise, what people say.
The truth is: the helpless have no respect.
People say it but you are silent.
You should speak too. The poor are not innocent.

Kind-hearted Madam, a day will soon dawn
when we shall have to re-evaluate the measures of life.
I can swear by my misery. I can swear by your greatness.
We shall have to revisit what is worthy of respect.

We have borne the brunt of degradation.
But we brought illumination to the face of time.
We have suffered the pain and stress of hard work.
But we have brought henna for the hands of time.

What is the outcome of these bitter squabbles?
If people say it, they must be right.
My friends may not have learnt the civilized ways.
Humans may not be residing in my part of the world.

Maadaam

aap bevajaha pareshaan si kyun hain maadaam
log kahte hain to phir thiik hi kahte hon ge
mere ahbaab ne tahziib n siikhi ho gi
mere maahaul mein insaan n rahte hon ge

nuur-e sarmaaya se hai ruu-e tamaddan ki jila
ham jahaan hain vahaan insaan n rahte hon ge
muflisi hisse lataafat ko mita sakti hai
bhuuk aadaab ke saanchon mein nahien dhal sakti

log kehte hain to logo p ta'ujjab kaisa
sach to kahte hain k naadaaron ki izzat kaisi
log kahte hain magar aap abhi tak chup kyun hain
aap bhi kahiye ghariibon mein sharaafat kaisi

nek maadaam! bahut jald voh daur aaye ga
jab hamein ziist ke advaar parakhne hon ge
apni zillat ki qasam aap ki azmat ki qasam
ham ko taa'ziim ke m'yiaar parakhne hon ge

ham ne har daur mein tazliil sahi hai lekin
ham ne har daur ke chehre ko zia bakhshi hai
ham ne har daur mein mehnat ke sitam jhiile hain
ham ne har daur ke haathon ko henna bakhshi hai

lekin in talkh mubahiss se bhala kiya haasil
log kehte hain to phir thiik hi kahte hon ge
mere ahbaab ne tahziib n siikhi ho gi
main jahaan huun vahaan insaan n rahte hon ge

A New Journey

This is a poem of heartfelt self-reflection and an effort to find purpose
or meaning in a new situation that life has created. The future is
uncertain. The past has not left much that the poet could be proud of.
Spring has come and gone and left behind nothing but grief. There is
darkness everywhere. Neither logic nor belief has served the purpose
that was promised. It is the same defeat and the same sorrow each
day. Friends, who were a great source of comfort, have moved away in
search of their own ports of call. The poem ends in the midst of great
uncertainty and doubt. Only one thing is known: it is a new journey
and what it entails has to be figured out.

Deceptive nets
of tomorrow's paradise
broke into pieces.
My life,
when it faces my longings,
is ashamed.
In the garden,
the celebration
of spring's arrival is over.
But the eyes of roses
and tulips show grief.

The dance of the whirlwind
is continuing.
In the horizon,
the blood-filled decanter
is still overflowing.
Where is the bright sun
and its illumination?
Darkness is showing
through the roof and the door.

The air outside is thinking:
what did the sons of Adam gain

by giving up reason
and testing preposterous beliefs?
It is the same defeat of one's desires
and the same sorrow each day.
What did the image of life
gain after losing everything?

My eyes wandered
in the vastness of hollow spheres
but they could not find
old witnesses of charm and beauty.
The long pathways came to an end
but I could not find the purpose
of my own journey.

My friends!
Keep on moving
because the journey has an end.
The old guides for our paths
will not turn their backs and look upon us.
When the sun rises,
the stars have to die.
Those who are in love with evenings,
they won't look this way.

Naya Safar

fareb-e jannat-e farda ke jaal tuut gaye
hayaat apni ummiidon p sharamsaar si hai
chaman mein jashn-e varuud-e bahaar ho bhi chuka
magar nigaah-e gul o laala sogvaar si hai

faza mein garm baguulon ka raqs jaari hai
ufaq p khuun ki miina chhalak rahi hai abhi
kahaan ka mahr-e munavvar kahaan ki tanviirein
k baam o dar p siyaahi jhalak rahi hai abhi

fazaayein soch rahi hain k ibn-e aadam ne
khirad ganva ke junuun aazma ke kya paaya
vohi shikast-e tamanna vohi gham-e ayyaam
nigaar-e ziist ne sab kuchh luta ke kya paaya

bhatak ke rah gayein nazrein khala ki vus'at mein
hariim-e shaahid-e ra'na ka kuchh pata n mila
taviil rahguzaar khatm ho gayi lekin
hanuuz apni masafat ka muntaha n mila

safar-nasiib rafiqo! qadam barhaaye chalo
puraane raah-numa laut kar n dekhein ge
tulu'-e sub-h se taaron ki maut hoti hai
shabon ke raaj-dulaare idhar n dekhein ge

Oppressed Masses and Revolutionary Change

Speaking to and for the oppressed workers and farmers was at the very core of the Progressive Writers' Movement. The poets in the movement were not writing to comfort the wounds inflicted by a tyrannical foreign regime. They were preparing the oppressed to hold aloft the banner of revolution—and bring about a radical political and social change that would make a total break with the past. In this regard, Sahir was no different. His poems, included in this section, were giving words to the sufferings of working folk, and offering them hope that their day in the sun, when they would become free of all forms of exploitation, would come soon.

My Songs

In this poem the poet sets aside the personal and goes directly to the collective. He says that it is not that love is not desirable, or that images of nature do not bring him satisfaction. It's that there are issues bigger than the demands and needs of one person: there is war and conflict; there are farmers who are struck by hunger; there are women who suffer inhuman treatment; there are youngsters who have lost hope in the future. These problems are compounded by sharp inequalities of wealth. Under these circumstances, what should be the subject of the poet's work? Could it be the love that he cherishes or the visions of natural beauty that move his heart? Or something else entirely?

After listening
to my rebellious songs
people think
that my heart has developed
a passionate dislike for love songs;
that I derive satisfaction
from war and conflict;
that my nature is suited
to liking stories of bloodshed;
that in my world
there is no time for dance
or melody;
that my beloved song
is the raucous rhythm
of rebellion.

But if they look
at the plight of my blazing nights;
or when I fix my gaze
on the stars and cry;
or when forgotten affairs show up
as images in my memory.
The intensity of the pain
exasperates me for hours.
When the force of longings
deeply resting in my dreams
wakes me up, I find my life
sitting alongside death.

Because I am a poet,
I am deeply attracted

to the wonders of nature,
and my heart as such
can never turn against
songs and melodies.
Nature has also taught me
love of mankind.
My purpose in life
could not be limited
to writing blazing songs.
I am young and, as we know,
youth is the tempest of missteps.
My conversation cannot be limited
to the colours of virtue and chastity.

The reality of my rebellious songs
can be limited to this:
that when I see farmers
struck by hunger, and folks
who are poor and helpless,
tender women in tears
and agonized youngsters,
atrocities unleashed by governments
and institutions,
when I compare the torn garments
of the many with the royal treasures of some,
my heart cannot come to grips
with the thoughts of assemblies of pleasure.
Even if I like it, I cannot sing
dream-inducing songs.

Mere Giit

mere sarkash taraane sun ke duniya y samajhti hai
k shaayad mere dil ko i'shq ke naghmon se nafrat hai
mujhe hangaama-e jung o jadal mein kaif milta hai
meri fitrat ko khuun-rezi ke afsaanon se raghbat hai

meri duniya mein kuchh vuq'at nahien hai raqs o naghma ki
mera mahbuub naghma shor-e aahang-e baghaavat hai

magar ai kaash dekhein voh meri pur-soz raaton ko
main jab taaron p nazrein gaar kar aansu bahaata huun
tasavvur ban ke bhuuli vaardaatein yaad aati hain
to soz o dard ki shiddat se pahron tilmilaata huun
koi khwaabon mein khwabiida ummangon ko jagaati hai
to apni zindagi ko maut ke pahlu mein paata huun

main shaa'yir huun mujhe fitrat ke nazzaaron se ulfat hai
mera dil dushman-e naghma-saraayi ho nahien sakta
mujhe insaaniyat ka dard bhi bakhsha hai kudrat ne
mera maqsad faqat sho'ala navaayi ho nahien sakta
javaan huun main javaani laghzishon ka ek tuufaan hai
meri baaton mein rang-e paarsaayi ho nahien sakta

mere sarkash taraanon ki haqiiqat hai to itni hai
k jab main dekhta huum bhuuk ke maare kisaanon ko
gharibon muflison ko be-kason ko be-saharon ko
sisakti naazniinon ko tarapte nau-javaanon ko
hukumat ke tashaddud ko imaaraat ke takabbur ko
kisi ke chiitharon ko aur shahanshaahi khazaanon ko

to dil taab-e nashaat-e bazme-e i'shrat la nahien sakta
main chaahun bhi to khwaab-aavar taaraane ga nahien sakta

Let Me Think

This is a 'making sense of the senseless' sort of poem. Life has become bitter poison. Why has everything gone wrong? The poet ponders these questions but gets no answers. Then there is a realization that the rest of the world is in no better state. There is fear and starvation. There is hunger and thirst. There is darkness all around. The poet then recognizes that it is the capitalist economic system that takes away from the poor and gives to the rich that is to be blamed. While the farmers work hard, they are unable to feed their own; while labourers toil in the smoke-emitting factories, they are caught up in the clasp of poverty. On the side of the town where the affluent live, life looks different. There are luxuries that the poor can't even think of. Why is it like this, asks the poet. He even points a finger at the gods people worship. What starts as a record of personal failing becomes a searing political and economic statement. While the model of economic salvation in the form of the Soviet Union that the progressives promoted lies buried in the heap of history, the truth of gross economic inequalities is still an important issue that the capitalist system has failed to resolve. Thus, Sahir's message has not lost its relevance.

Don't repeat the story
of my failed love affair.
Don't tell me
the tale of your failed longings.
Life is bitter, life is poison,
life is venom.
It is sickness, it is coercion,
it is filled with sorrow.
But look at the scale of pain
and grief.
Look at the masses
who are losing their breath
in the shadow of oppression.
Don't tell me the tale
of your failed longings.
Don't repeat the story
of my failed love affair.

Throngs of frightened people
seen in the gatherings.
Groups of starving people
standing at crossroads.
Land withered and blackened
by hunger and thirst.

The sick and poor living in dark homes.
The new human facing the battle
between capital and toil.
Nations fighting
under the banner
of peace and civility.
Everywhere, a great flood of fire
is melting iron.
The world is always dividing itself
in fashionable ways.

Fields filled with flowing greenery
provide a youthful look,
and in the farmer's house
there is no light or smoke.
These mills kissing the sky
and these alluring silvery white bazaars.
Hungry and helpless people
pouncing on dirt.

A line of bright and shiny homes
seen near the ocean in some distance.
Behind the rustle of curtains
a collection of beds of roses.
Doors and windows flooded
with white lights—
like a drunken poet's creation
of a world in his dreams.
Why is it like this? What is it?
Let me think.
Who is the god
that humans worship?
Let me think.

Don't tell me the tale
of your failed longings.

Don't repeat the story
of my failed love affair.

Mujhe Sochne Do

meri naakaam mohabbat ki kahaani mat chher
apni maayuus umangon ka fasaana n suna
zindagi talkh sahi zahr sahi sam hi sahi
dard-o aazaar sahi jabr sahi gham hi sahi
lekin is dard o gham o jabr ki vus'at ko to dekh
zulm ki chhaanv mein dam torti khalqat ko to dekh
apni maayuus umangon ka fasaana n suna
meri naakaam mohabbat ki kahaani mat chher

jalsa-gaahon mein y dahshat-zada sahme amboh
rahguzaaron p falaakat-zada logon ke giroh
bhuuk aur pyaas se pazh-murda siyah-faam zamiin
tira o taar makaan muflis o biimaar makiin
nau-e insaan mein y sarmaaya o mehnat ka tazaad
amn o tahziib ke parcham tale qaumon ka fasaad
har taraf aatish o aahan ka y sailaab-e aziim
nit-naye tarz p hoti hui duniya taqsiim

lahlahaate huye kheton p javaani ka samaan
aur dahqaan ke chhappar mein n batti n dhuaan
y falak-bos millein dilkash o siimiin baazaar
y ghalaazat p jhapat-te hue bhuuke naadaar

duur saahil p voh shaffaf makaanon ki qataar
sarsaraate huye pardon mein simat-te gulzaar
dar o diivaar p anvaar ka sailaab ravaan
jaise ik sha'ayar-e madhosh ke khwabon ka jahaan
y sabhi kyun hai y kya hai mujhe kuchh sochne de

apni maayuus umangon ka fasaana n suna
meri naakaam mohabbat ki kahaani mat chher

The New Year Morning

The rich and poor lead very different lives. This is not something new. But Sahir points to a particular aspect of the rich–poor social divide and that has to do with their social engagements—how they celebrate some festive occasions that mean little to people on the other side. While for the poor traditional festivals like Diwali and Holi hold great attraction, the rich have acquired a fascination for some new things, like celebrating the start of a new calendar year. For the poor, life is an endless struggle for survival. The poet paints a picture that is tragic as well as satirical. A New Year celebration is underway: the roads are beautified; gifts are being exchanged. For the poor it is like any other day. A farmer's daughter is coming out of a mansion after selling her body for someone's pleasure for a few bucks. Hungry kids are running after automobiles. Nothing is different for these people. The New Year's morning is a grim reminder of a social malady the roots of which lie in gross wealth inequalities.

Rays of light ruptured the East.
The present became a story of the past and
it echoed the melody of the future.
Friends have sent gifts, but there is dust
gathered in the corners of the table.
The roads are beautified
like a newly married woman.
Celebrate the New Year!

A poor farmer's daughter
walked out of the front door of a mansion.
Miserable, shrivelled,
nursing the pain in her joints.
Trying to cover her bosom with her scarf.
Clutching a currency note in her fist.
Celebrate the New Year!

Hungry beggar kids,
running after an automobile.
Hurt by an awareness that came before time.
Rubbing their pus-laden eyes;
scratching boils on their heads.
Lo, some more appeared on the scene.
Celebrate the New Year!

Sub-he Nauroz

phuut pariin mashriq se kirnein
haal bana maazi ka fasaana
guunja mustaqabil ka taraana
bheje hain ahbaab ne tohfe
atay pare hain mez ke kone
dulhan bani hui hain raahein
jashn manaao saal-e nau ke

nikli hai bangle ke dar se
ik muflis dahqaan ki beti
afsurda murjhaaii hui si
jism ke dukhte jor dabaati
aanchal se siine ko chhupaati
mutthi mein ik note dabaaye
jashn manaao saal-e nau ke

bhuuke zard gadaagar bachche
kaar ke piichhe bhaag rahe hain
vaqt se pehle jaag uthe hain
piip bhari aankhein sahlaate
sar ke phoron ko khujlaate
voh dekho kuchh aur bhi nikle
jashn manaao saal-e nau ke

A Blessed Moment

This is a short poem that aims to highlight some disturbing developments in the western hemisphere. A war between imperialist and fascist forces has brought about destruction on a vast scale. There is ideological division within the imperialist camp as well. The poet's message is simple: do not worry, oppressed masses, because the oppressors are suffering in their own way, and possibly this would be good news for you.

Smile, my motherland, covered in darkness.
Raise your head, my oppressed masses.
Look near the western horizon
where winds look like a whirling vortex.
Men in old gambling houses
are arguing like old chess players.
No one is keeping an eye on you.
These heavy, cold chains—
they are rusted, though made of iron.
There is a chance that they would break today.
Breathe, it is a blessed moment, my dear friend!
Raise your head, my oppressed masses.

Lamha-e Ghanimat

muskara ai zamiin-e tiira o taar
sar utha ai dabi hui makhluuq
dekh voh maghribi ufaq ke qariib
aandhiyaan pech o taab khaane lagiin
aur puraane qimaar khaane mein
kohna shaatir baham ulajhne lage
koi teri taraf nahien nigraan
y giraanbaar sard zanjiirein
zang khurda hain aahani hi sahi
aaj mauq'a hai tuut sakti hain
fursat-e yak nafas ghanimat jaan
sar utha ai dabi makhluuq

My Songs are Your Songs

This is a poem of dedication, devotion to the cause of the workers'
revolution. Gone are the days when the poet sang songs of love and
love's ordeals. There is a new challenge. Workers can't fight their battle
against capital on their own. They need a partner—a songster to inspire
them, to keep them going. And the poet is ready to dedicate his self and
his songs to their cause, and he does it with a great deal of passion.

Until now
my songs carried hope
and a sense of defeat.
They had the sound
of the footsteps of death
and a relaxed view of life.
They held the rays of tomorrow
and the heavily burdened darkness
of the present.
They had the noise of tempests
and the soothing music
of dreams.

But from today onwards,
my poetry will have sparks of fire.
Within the soft, free-flowing tunes
I would fill it with streams of life.
On life's darkened paths,
I would appear with a torch in my hand.
The vastly spread out scarf of my land,
I would fill it with red stars.

From today onwards,
O labourers and farmers,
my songs are your songs.
O starving folk,
my destiny is now one with yours.

Until the time you are hungry
and you have no clothes to wear
my songs will not be silenced.
As long as you are distressed,
my songs shall not be used
just for one's comfort.

I don't care
if people refuse to consider me
a poet or an artist.
The traders of thought and fun
might not consider my couplets
worth anything.
From today onwards,
I dedicate my art and my hopes
to you.
From today onwards,
my songs are a reflection
of your pain and comfort.

Drawing strength from you,
I would show you the path.
My dear companion,
you should unfurl the flag
and I will sing a song on a harp.
From today onwards,
the purpose of my art is to melt
the chains.
From today onwards,
I would rain sparks
instead of dew.

Mere Giit Tumhaare Hain

ab tak mere giiton mein ummid bhi thi paspaayii bhi
maut ke qadmon ki aahat bhi jiivan ki angraayii bhi

mustaqbil ki kirnein bhi thiin haal ki bojhal zulmat bhi
tuufaanon ka shor bhi tha aur khwabon ki shahnaayii bhi

aaj se main apne giiton mein aatish-paare bhar duun ga
maddham lachkiili taanon mein jiivat dhaare bhar duun ga
jiivan ke andhiyaare path par mish'al le kar nikluun ga
dharti ke phaile aanchal mein surkh sitaare bhar duun ga

aaj se ai mazduur kisaano! mere giit tumhaare hain
faaqa-kash insaano! mere jog-bahaag tumhaare hain
jab tak tum bhuuke nange ho y sho'le khaamosh n honge
jab tak be-aaraam ho tum y naghme raahat-kosh n honge

mujh ko is ka ranj nahien hai log mujhe fankaar n maanein
fikr o fan ke taajir mere she'yron ko ash'aar n maanein
mera fan meri ummidein aaj se tum ko arpan hain
aaj se mere giit tumhaare dukh aur sukh ka darpan hain

tum se quvvat le kar ab main tum ko raah dikhauun ga
tum parcham lahraana saathi main barbat par gauun ga
aaj se mere fan ka maqsad zanjiirein pighlaana hai
aaj se main shabnam ke badle angaare barsauun ga

Against Oppression

This poem raises the question about the best way to fight oppression.
Advocating war against the oppressor is against the Gandhian
approach of meeting violence with non-violence. But since progressives
like Sahir owed allegiance to the communist ideology, their poetry
often advocated blood for blood, bullet for bullet. There is a twist here
about the nature of the war itself. It is not just a war for freedom; it is
a war against capitalism (class warfare) in which violence was justified
by communist leaders like Lenin, Mao, and Castro.

We want peace
but if it is essential to fight oppression

using war as a tool, then so be it.
The one who does not stop oppression,
he stands with the oppressors.
The one who does not stop killing,
he is the killer's buddy.
We have risen, putting our life at risk
to ensure that justice prevails.
Tell the one who supports
the forces of wrongdoing:
If that is where you want to go,
welcome!

The oppressor has no caste, no faith,
no national identity.
On the oppressor's lips
any mention of these is a sin.
The branch of tyranny
does not flourish on this land.
History makes it clear
and time is a witness.
Those who are inwardly blind
do not understand

that this is capital's war;
it is not about farm lands.
This war is about principles of awakening.
The blood that we have offered to this land,
that blood is food for the roses.
The dawn of peace will break out,
though dipped in the colour of blood.

Magar Zulm Ke Khilaaf

ham amn chaahte hain magar zulm ke khilaaf
gar jung laazmi hai to phir jang hi sahi

zaalim ko jo n roke voh shaamil hai zulm mein
qaatil ko jo n toke voh qaatil ke saath hai
ham sar ba kaf uthe hain k haq fata-h yaab ho
kah do use jo lashkar-e baatil ke saath hai
is dhang par hai zor to y dhang hi sahi

zaalim ki koi zaat n mazhab n koi qaum
zaalim ke lab p zikr bhi in ka gunaah hai
phalti nahien hai shaakh-e sitam is zamiin par
taariikh jaanti hai zamaana gavaah hai
kuchh kor-baatinon ki nazar tang hi sahi

y zar ki jang hai n zamiinon ki jang hai
y jang hai baqa ke usuulon ke vaaste
jo khuun ham ne nazar diya hai zamiin ko
voh khuun hai gulaab ke phuulon ke vaaste
phuutegi sub-he amn lahuu-rang hi sahi

Blood, After All, Is Blood

Patrice Lumumba was chosen the first prime minister of the newly independent African nation of Congo in 1960. But soon thereafter there was an attempted coup in the country supported by Belgium, its former colonizer. The ensuing crisis brought Cold War rivals, the United States and the Soviet Union, face-to-face. When Lumumba sought help from the Soviet Union to avert the crisis, the pro-Western chief of army staff, General Mobutu, arrested him, and the young prime minister was executed by a firing squad. This cowardly act was strongly condemned by people around the world.

Incidentally, there was an international peace conference in Delhi around this time. Several progressive poets and writers like Ali Sardar Jafri, Sajjad Zaheer, K.A. Abbas, Jan Nisar Akhtar, and Sahir were participating in the conference. There was a poetical symposium scheduled for one of the evenings. Jafri asked Sahir to take the lead and write a poem about Lumumba's assassination. Sahir replied that he had not thought about it. But Jafri was not ready to give up easily. He brought a chicken sandwich, a bottle of beer, and a pack of cigarettes for Sahir and locked him in his hotel room, telling him, 'I would like to see the poem when I open the door four hours from now.' This plan worked. The result was the best revolutionary poem Sahir ever wrote.[13]

The oppressor can draw blood in different ways—through torture, by killing, by dismembering bodies. But the blood of those who are tormented is not something passive. It has life of its own. Once drawn, it becomes a testament to the oppressor's cowardliness, a weapon that brings about the oppressor's downfall. A quote attributed to Jawaharlal Nehru has him saying that 'a dead Lumumba is much more powerful than the living Lumumba.' Sahir's poem is a strong example of reality transformed into symbolism. This is one of those poems that should be read more than once, and read aloud.

Oppression,
if taken to its limits,
quashes itself.
Blood, after all, is blood.
If you spill it,
it will clot.

Whether it clots
in sandy deserts
or on the hand of a murderer;
whether it congeals
for want of justice
or on feet bound in chains;
whether it dries
on the sword of tyranny
or on the body of the slaughtered—

---

[13] Varma and Abid, *Main Sahir Huun*, 212.

Blood, after all, is blood.
If you spill it,
it will curdle.

One could try
to stow away in hideouts.
Blood itself points
to the dwelling places
of the killers.
Conspiracies might proceed
to take away darkness's disguise.
Each drop
when it falls on the palm of one's hand
is a candle of light.

Speak to the good-for-nothing
fate of oppression.
Speak to the power
in the compass of wisdom.
Speak to Laila[14]
seated in the assembly of nations.

Blood is crazy,
it can grab the end
of your garment.
It is a violent ball of flame
and it can collect the harvest.

You tried to suppress blood
at the executioner's post.
Now it has appeared

---

[14] Laila, a symbol of love and beauty, is drawn from the classic love
story *Laila-Majnun*, where the eponymous characters rise above the hatred
between their families and fall in love with each other.

on the streets and in the market places,
looking like a flame, a slogan,
a stone.

When blood gets tricky,
bayonets can't stop it.
When it raises its head,
you can't subdue it
with mirrors.

What can we say about tyranny,
what can we say about its station!
Tyranny is just tyranny
from beginning to end.
Blood, after all, is blood,
it can appear in one hundred forms.
Such forms
that you can't just erase them.
Such flames
that you can't just douse them.
Such slogans
that you can't just squash them.

Khuun Phir Khuun Hai

zulm phir zulm hai barhta hai to mit jaata hai
khuun phir khuun hai tapke ga to jam jaaye ga

khaake sahra p jame ya kaf-e qaatil p jame
farq-e insaaf p ya paa-e salaasil p jame
tegh-e bedaad p ya laasha-e bismal p jame
khuun phir khuun hai tapke ga to jam jaaye ga

laakh baithe koi chhup chhup ke kamiin gaahon mein
khuun khud deta hai jalladon ke maskan ka suraagh

saazishein laakh urati rahein zulmat ki naqaab
le ke har buund nikalti hai hatheli p charaagh

zulm ki qismat-e naakaara o rusva se kaho
jabr ki hikmat-e parkaar ke iima se kaho
mahmil-e majlis-e aqvaam ki laila se kaho

khuun diivaana hai daaman p lapak sakta hai
sho'la-e tund hai khirman p lapak sakta hai

tum ne jis khuun ko maqtal mein dabaana chaaha
aaj vo kuucha o bazaar mein aa nikla hai
kahin sh'ola kahiin na'ara kahiin patthar ban kar

khuun chalta hai to rukta nahien sangiinon se
sar uthaata hai koi to dabta nahien aaiinon se

zulm ki baat hi kya zulm ki auqaat hi kya
zulm bas zulm hai aaghaaz se anjaam talak
khuun phir khuun hai sau shakl badal sakta hai
aisi shaklein k mitaao to mitaae n bane
aise sh'ole k bujhaao to bujhaae n bane
aaise na'are k dabaao to dabaae n bane

The Voice of Man

This is a typical progressive poem that extols the virtues of the
working man—his ability to place his physical strength in the objects
of his creation, his dedication to be the best in whatever he does.
But in the capitalist system, his voice is suppressed. He is denied fair
compensation for his work. But there is hope. The guardians of the
old system are having a 'farewell feast' and as the new dawn with
the 'pomegranate flag flying on its shoulders' breaks, the voice of man
will be heard loud and clear.

We shall see how long the voice of man
is suppressed;

How long angry emotions are stopped
from surfacing.
Our limitations apart,
how long will the rule of tyranny last?

From the doors of prison houses
or from the heights of the gallows,
we shall see your notoriety
in worldly places,
though we may have to wait a little bit.
We shall see in the end
our glory and drunken celebrations.

You should see the vanity of power
built on frames of iron and steel.
We shall see the kindness and goodness of spirit.
We shall see the face of one who wears
his useless cap merrily.

Fair compensation for work
is part of human history and tradition.
Let us see for how long
you shoot arrows.
How long this tyranny shall last,
let us see.

The sons of darkness are having a farewell feast.
We shall see the pomegranate flag
on the shoulders of the coming day.
You will have to see this;
And to this, we shall see!

Aavaaz-e Aadam

dabe gi kab talak aavaaz-e aadam ham bhi dekhein ge
rukein ge kab talak jazbaat-e barham ham bhi dekhein ge
chalo yuunhi sahi y jaur-e paiham ham bhi dekhein ge

dar-e zindaan se dekhein ya uruuj-e daar se dekhein
tumhein rusva sar-e baazaar-e aa'lam ham bhi dekhein ge
zara dam lo ma-aal-e shaukat-e jam ham bhi dekhein ge

y zo'am-e quvvat-e faulaad o aahan dekh lo tum bhi
befaiz-e jazba-e imaan-e mohkam ham bhi dekhein ge
jabiin-e kaj kulaahi khaak par kham ham bhi dekhein ge

mukaafaat-e amal taariikh-e insaan ki rivaayat hai
karoge kab talak naavak faraaham ham bhi dekhein ge
kahaan tak hai tumhaare zulm mein dam ham bhi dekhein ge

y hangaam-e vid'a-e shab hai ai zulmat ke farzando
sahar ke dosh par gulnaar parcham ham bhi dekhein ge
tumhein bhi dekhna hoga y aa'lam ham bhi dekheinge

The Feudal Order

Sahir was born to a landlord's family. But he was removed from that environment by his mother when he was very young. It is therefore unlikely that he had had first-hand experience of what life in such a milieu is like. But he must have heard stories from his mother and his friends. This must have given him a fairly good picture of the lecherous lifestyle of most landlords, who treated women and girls from poor farming families as their property, using them for sexual gratification. Sahir knew that his father had ten other wives before he married his mother. The poems in this section paint a picture of the feudal order that fortunately ended after Independence with the enforcement of various land reform initiatives.

The Land of Despair

This is a poem of grief and remembrance, melancholy and despair. The poet strikes a note of sadness in the opening lines and this feeling of despondency is carried throughout the text. It starts with personal reflections and memories of meetings with friends who are no longer with him. This flow of past memories brings back visions of neighbourhoods where once he had lived and cheerful days of his college life, including memories of 'Venus-like' beauties he had known. These images pinch the poet's heart. Then the focus shifts to the maidens of his village who had to suffer indignities because of the poverty of their parents. The pain in the poem is thereby no longer a personal pain. It becomes a collective dirge—about the suffering inflicted by the land on its own people. When he meets these maidens in the street, the poet lowers his head with shame. What started as a personal loss thus becomes a manifestation of social and political malaise. Sahir is well known for using this transformative technique in his poems, and he does it with such flair that he never loses the emotional involvement of the reader.

I'm sick of living.
Every breath that I take is a sign of illness.
How melancholic is life!
How despairing is life!
My meetings with fellow countrymen—
those poetry-loving folks—
when I remember them
my heart shuts down.
Pleasant memories that are history now.
The hobbies that are lost for good.
These things make me cry for hours.
It is a thorn in my flesh.
Those tremors of joy and chirpings;
the soul-nourishing laughter.
That was a time when my heart was still alive.
There were no clouds of senselessness.
Those colourful vales of college life!
Neighbourhoods that had heart in them.
Those maidens of my land.
Those native beauties with Venus-like foreheads.
Their colourful dresses breathing fire

And—to top it all—their fiery speech.
Their friendly love
and the colours of their familiar credence.
They gave to my failed heart,
blood-stained wanderer,
a mark of separation and
took away my divinity.
In remembrance of those moments,
in remembrance of those small joys,
I am always grieving.
I bear the pain of suffering.
When friends share
their stories of sorrow,
I get restless,
I get lost in my own sighs.
Those friends and relatives
who broke the promise of constancy,
who turned their faces away from those whom they loved,
who severed their relationship with the world,
they disappeared to the other side of the horizon,
to the other side of the rainbow,
in a valley of silence
in a state of unconsciousness.
They went to sleep in the depths of valleys
and they were lost in darkness.
These images appear unexpectedly
and they pinch my heart,
and I suffer tears of blood,
becoming restless.
Those maidens of my village,
the unfortunate daughters of farmers,
suffering excesses of despair and
abject poverty,
they lost their chastity and
honour, and they lost themselves.

Their youth turned into a sad chapter and
a tale of infamy.
When I come face-to-face with them
in the village lanes,
I lower my eyes.
I try to hide myself.
How melancholic is life!
How despairing is life!

Sar Zamiin-e Yaas

jiine se dil bezaar hai
har saans ik aazaar hai
kitni haziin hai zindagi
andoh-giin hai zindagi
voh bazm-e ahbaab-e vatan
voh ham navaayaan-e sukhan
aate hain jis dam yaad ab
karte hain dil naashaad ab
guzri hui rangiiniyaan
khoii hui dilchaspiyaan
pahron rulaati hain mujhe
aksar sataati hain mujhe
voh zamzame voh chahchahe
voh ruuh-afza qahqahe
jab dil ko maut aayi na thi
yuun behisi chhaayi na thi
kollej ki rangiin vaadiyaan
voh dil nashiin aabaadiyaan
voh naazninaan-e vatan
zohra jabiinan-e vatan
jin mein se ik rangiin qaba
aatish nafs aatish nava
kar ke mohabbat aashna
rang-e a'qidat aashna
mere dil-e naakaam ko

khuun-gashta-e aalaam ko
daagh-e judaayi de gayi
saari khudaayi le gayi
in saa'yaton ki yaad mein
in rahton ki yaad mein
maghmuum sa rahta huun main
gham ki kasak sahta huun main
sunta huun jab ahbaab se
qisse gham-e ayyaam ke
betaab ho jaata huun main
aahon mein kho jaata huun main
phir voh aziz-o aqriba
jo tor kar a'hd-e vafa
ahbaab se munh mor kar
duniya se rishta tor kar
hadd-e ufuq se us taraf
rang-e shafaq se us taraf
ik vaadii-e khaamosh ki
ik aa'lam-e behosh ki
gahraaiiyon mein sau gaye
taariikiyon mein kho gaye
un ka tasavvur naa-gahaan
leta hai dil mein chutkiyaan
aur khuun rulata hai mujhe
bekal banaata hai mujhe
voh gaanv ki ham-joliyaan
mafluuk dahqaan zaadiyaan
jo daste-e fart-e yaas se
aur yuurish-e aflaas se
ismat luta kar rah gayiin
khud ko ganva kar rah gayiin
ghamgiin javaani ban gayiin
rusava kahaani ban gayiin
un se kabhi galiyon mein ab
hota huun main do-chaar jab
nazrein jhuka leta huun main

khud ko chhupa leta huun main
kitni haziin hai zindagi
andoh-giin hai zindagi

Estate

If we are looking for a poem with a strong link to the poet's family experience, then 'Estate' makes the cut. Sahir's father was a *jagiirdaar* (landlord) whose family had received a large chunk of agricultural land as reward for loyalty to the British. As land provides income year after year, it promotes a luxuriant and lazy lifestyle on the part of its owner. Sahir's father had married one woman after another. Farmers who worked for the landlord were no better than indentured slaves: they had nowhere to go and the income they earned was hardly adequate for sustainable living. The exploitation of young girls and women was a common occurrence. As we read this poem, it becomes apparent why Sahir hated his father with such raw intensity.

Once again,
I have returned
to the valley of my youth
in which are concealed
the places of excitement
of my dreams.
For the sensual pleasures
of my dear friends
there are bright bosoms,
youthful bodies,
and delightful arms.

Damsels immersed
in the fields of greenery.
In their veins
who knows
whose blood runs.
Who has the courage

to acknowledge this?
Lips are sealed
with dreaded silence.

Ah! those sizzling
and tempting bosoms
giving us the gift
left behind for us
by our ancestors.
Wonder how these frail
and feeble farmers
give birth
to these snow-like bodies
in their darkened hearths!

Oh! these plants
that move to and fro
and these dazzling fields.
They once belonged
to my ancestors
and now they are mine.
These grazing fields,
these cattle, these animals,
and these farmers.
All of this is mine,
they are mine,
they are mine.

Their toil is mine
and the fruit of their labour
is mine too.
Their arms are mine
and so too
the produce of these arms.
I am the lord of this inheritance
without any question.

The pleasure of these cheeks
and the breeze of these tresses—
they belong to me.

I am the son
of forefathers
who have consistently supported
every move of foreign rulers.
With apologies
at every inauspicious moment
they have surrendered themselves
to the will of the rulers.

These fatigued structures
that crawl on this land,
with eyes that have never become
the sword of resistance.
Their lack of courage
can discourage anyone.
Arches of their eyebrows
have neither tightened
nor would they ever tighten.

Oh! the evening, these fountains,
and the reddish glow of the twilight!
Why don't I sway
in these comforting airs?
Who is noiselessly and softly
walking towards me?
Why don't I move forward
and kiss her chiselled lips?

Jaagiir

phir usi vaadi-e shaadaab mein laut aaya huun
jis mein pinhaan mere khwabon ki tarab-gaahein hain

mere ahbaab ke saamaan-e ta'ayyush ke liye
shokh siine hain javaan jism hasiin baanhein hain

sabz kheton mein y dubki hui doshiizaaein
in ki shiryaanon mein kis kis ka lahu jaari hai
kis mein jurrat hai k is raaz ki tashhiir kare
sab ke lab par meri haibat ka fusuun taari hai

haaye voh garm o dil-aavez ubalte siine
jin se ham satvat-e aaba ka sila lete hain
jaane un marmariin jimson ko y mariyal dahqaan
kaise in tiiraah gharondo mein janam dete hain

y lahakte hue paude y damakte hue khet
pahle ajdaad ki jaagiir the ab mere hain
y chara-gaah y revar y maveshi y kisaan
sab ke sab mere hain sab mere hain sab mere hain

in ki mehnat bhi meri haasil-e mehnat bhi mera
in ke baazu bhi mere quvvat-e baazu bhi meri
main khudaavand huun us vus'at-e be-paayan ka
mauj-e aa'riz bhi meri nikhat-e gesu bhi meri

main un ajdaad ka beta huun jinhon ne paiham
ajnabi qaum ke saaye ki himaayat ki hai
u'zr ki saa'at-e naapaak se le kar ab tak
har kare vaqt mein sarkaar ki khidmat ki hai

khaak par rengne vaale y fasurda dhaanche
in ki nazrein kabhi talvaar bani hain na banein
in ki ghairat p har ik haath jhapat sakta hai
in ke abru ki kamaanein n tani hain n tanein

haaye y shaam y jharne y shafaq ki laali
main in aasuuda fazaaon mein zara jhuum n luun
vo dabe paanv idhar kaun chali jaati hai
badh ke us shokh ke tarshe hue lab chuum n luun

Princes

Wealthy landlords, their connections with the British, and their abuse and exploitation of poor, landless farmers—this is an attack on the lazy and exploitative class of people brought into being by the British Raj, people who are unmindful of the coming revolution, of the warnings that their time is coming to an end. The poet ridicules them for their disconnection with the real world. He tells them: 'Go to sleep and sleep for a long time.'

Thinking of stories
of the greatness of your ancestors,
go away and get lost in the emptiness
of your dark nests,
go to sleep embracing
snow-white fairies.
Walk on pieces of floating clouds,
fly in the company of the moon and stars.
This is the legacy
that your ancestors have left for you.

Far away in the western hemisphere
is a brightly burning fire.
Not a machination
of those with capital.
It could be the war
between capital and labour.
It is in the West
but not in the eastern hemisphere.
What do you have to gain
from the West's complexities?

Darkness ended,
red streaks unrolled.
Melodies were heard in the West—
melodies of democracy, justice, and freedom.

On the eastern shores:
gaseous smoke is billowing up;
fire rained by unfamiliar guns;
the roofs of sleeping chambers start to crack.

Get up from your beds.
Show respect to your new masters.
After having done that,
go back into the emptiness of your nests.
Go to sleep and sleep for a long time.

Shaahzaade

zehn mein a'zmat-e ajdaad ke qisse le kar
apne taariik gharondon ke khala mein kho jaao
marmariin khwaabon ki pariyon se lipat kar so jaao
abr paaron p chalo chaand sitaron mein uro
yahi ajdaad se virse mein mila hai tum ko

duur maghrib ki fazaaon mein dahakti hui aag
ahl-e sarmaaya ki aavezish-e baaham n sahi
jang-e sarmaaya o mehnat hi sahi
duur maghrib mein hai mashriq ki faza mein to nahien
tum ko maghrib ke bakheron se bhala kya lena

tiirgi khatm hui surkh shua'ayein phailiin
duur maghrib ki fazaaon mein taraane guunje
fat-h-e jamhuur ke insaaf ke aazaadi ke
saahil-e sharq p gaison ka dhuaan chhaane laga
aag barsaane lage ajnabi topon ke dahan
khwaab-gaahon ki chhatein girne lagiin

apne bistar se utho
naye aaqaaon ki taaziim karo
aur phir apne gharondon ke khala mein kho jaao
tum bahut der bahut der talak soye raho

Exploitation of Women

Given the situation of his own mother, Sahir paid attention to the treatment of women in Indian society and used his poetic skills to create awareness of the injustice that they suffer. Men make the rules that women have to obey. Men use religious dogmas that support their viewpoints. Women have no recourse except to suffer the consequences of an unjust social and religious order framed for them. The law of the land claims to protect them in theory, but in practice justice often remains elusive for women.

Woman

This poem, which was used by Guru Dutt in 1957 for his film *Pyaasa,* touched the conscience of the nation with its refrain. Much has changed since then. There are more women who have gained access to education and productive employment. Yet, greater progress is needed for eradicating prostitution, ensuring equal pay for equal work, and expanding educational opportunities for girls in the rural areas, among other things. The future promises greater developmental avenues for girls and women, but credit goes to Sahir for highlighting this sensitive issue when silence on the topic was the norm.

Woman gave birth to men,
they gave her
a place to sell herself.

Suppressed at will,
rebuked at will.
Weighed in dinars
and sold in markets.
Made to dance naked
in the courts of amusement.
This is that disregarded one
who is sought by the highly esteemed.

They do not feel shy
in getting a piece of her.

Woman gave birth to men,
they gave her
a place to sell herself.

Men get away with
anything,
the woman is at fault
even for crying.
Men seek enjoyment
the way they want it,
but woman is punished
just for the sin
of being alive.
Men have quarters
to delight themselves,
woman has one place for sure—
the cremation ground.

Woman gave birth to men,
they gave her
a place to sell herself.

Men traded the bosoms
that nurtured them
and the womb that shaped
their bodies.
The body from which they sprouted
like a bud
is an object of scorn.

Woman gave birth to men,
they gave her
a place to sell herself.

When poverty nourishes
flagrancy,
the path from hunger
goes straight to the whorehouse.
Man's lust is laundered
in woman's sin.

Woman gave birth to men,
they gave her
a place to sell herself.

Woman is the world's fate,
yet her own fate is doomed.
She gives birth to saints
and prophets,
yet she herself is called
the devil's offspring.
She is the ill-fated mother
who is stretched out
for pleasure
on her offspring's
sleeping places.

Woman gave birth to men,
they gave her
a place to sell herself.

Aurat

aurat ne janam diya mardon ko mardon ne use baazaar diya
jab bhi chaaha masla kuchla jab bhi chaaha dhutkaar diya

tulti hai kahiin diinaaron mein bikti hai kahiin baazaaron mein
nangi nachvaayi jaati hai ayyaashon ke darbaaron mein
y vo be-izzat chiiz hai jo bat jaati hai izzat-daaron mein
aurat ne janam diya mardon ko mardon ne use baazaar diya

mardon ke liye har zulm rava aurat ke liye rona bhi khata
mardon ke liye har a'ish ka haq aurat ke liye jiina bhi saza
mardon ke liye laakhon sejein aurat ke liye bas ek chita
aurat ne janam diya mardon ko mardon ne use baazaar diya

jin siinon ne in ko duudh diya un siinon ko bevpaar kiya
jis kokh mein in ka jism dhala us kokh ka kaarobaar kiya
jis tan se uge konpal ban kar us tan ko zalil o khvaar kiya
aurat ne janam diya mardon ko mardon ne use baazaar diya

sansaar ki har ik be-sharmi ghurbat ki god mein palti hai
chaklon hi mein aa kar rukti hai faaqon se jo raah nikalti hai
mardon ki havas hai jo aksar aurat ke paap mein dhalti hai
aurat ne janam diya mardon ko mardon ne use baazaar diya

aurat sansaar ki qismat hai phir bhi taqdiir ki heti hai
autaar payambar jannati hai phir bhi shaitaan ki beti hai
ye vo bad-qismat maan hai jo beton ki sej p leti hai
aurat ne janam diya mardon ko mardon ne use bazaar diya

Whorehouses

This poem, also in *Pyaasa*, had a very broad social impact. Even Prime
Minister Nehru said that he was moved by this poem and its depiction
in the film. It is a darkly descriptive poem. The poet takes the reader
through narrow lanes, winding, dimly lit, and foul-smelling streets
where human flesh is bought and sold. The scene inside the rooms is
described with great realism. Floral bangles, laughter, spittle, the sound
of drums, hands stretching to grab bosoms—this collage of images
makes the reader visually grasp the tragedy these helpless victims
suffer. There is no escape for them. The refrain used in this poem
('Defenders of the sanctity of the East—where are they?') is a direct hit
at the leaders of religious and moral establishments who never stop
pontificating but who sadly avert their gaze from the plight of women
and young girls. The poet does not spare an opportunity to shame them.
It is because of poems like these that Sahir will always be remembered

as a champion of women's rights, particularly the right to lead lives free of exploitation.

These narrow lanes,
these auction houses of attractions.
These caravans of life
that are being looted.
Where are the guardians
of our pride?
Those defenders of the sanctity of the East—
where are they?

These winding streets
and these dreamless bazaars.
These strange travellers
and the jingle of coins.
The deals of chastity
and bargains that are struck.
Those defenders of the sanctity of the East—
where are they?

These foul-smelling, dimly lit,
narrow streets.
These crushed, half-opened yellow shoots.
These empty amusements for sale.
Those defenders of the sanctity of the East—
where are they?

The tinkle of anklets
from lighted windows.
The sound of a drum
concealing confused breaths.
People clearing throats in soulless rooms.
Those defenders of the sanctity of the East—
where are they?

Loud laughter stalking pathways.
Crowds staring at the windows.
Sounds following the edges of scarves.
Those defenders of the sanctity of the East—
where are they?

Floral bangles
and drool falling from mouths.
Ogling glances
and audacious bantering.
Decaying bodies
and disease-eaten faces.
Those defenders of the sanctity of the East—
where are they?

Hungry looks
at beautiful girls.
Hands stretching,
trying to grab bosoms.
Jumping feet
chasing staircases.
Those defenders of the sanctity of the East—
where are they?

The old and young—
they have all been here.
Healthy sons and ageing fathers.
She is a wife, a sister,
and a mother.
Those defenders of the sanctity of the East—
where are they?

Eve's daughter is asking for help.
Someone like Yashodha,
Radha's daughter.
One of the Prophet's followers,

and Zulekha's daughter.
Those defenders of the sanctity of the East—
where are they?

Send for the country's leaders and guides.
Show them these lanes, these streets,
and these spectacles.
Bring the defenders
of the sanctity of the East here.
Where are the defenders
of the sanctity of the East?

Chakle

y kuuche y nilaam ghar dilkashi ke
y lut-te hue kaarvaan zindagi ke
kahaan hain kahaan hain muhaafiz khudi ke
sanaa-khwaan-e taqdiis-e mashriq kahaan hain

y pur-pech galiyaan y be-khwaab baazaar
y gumnaam raahi y sikkon ki jhankaar
y ismat ke saude y saudon p takraar
sanaa-khwaan-e taqdiis-e mashriq kahaan hain

taa'ffun se pur-niim raushan y galiyaan
y masli hui adh khili zard kaliyaan
y bikti hui khokhli rang raliyaan
sana-khwaan-e taqdiis-e mashriq kahaan hain

voh ujle dariichon mein paayal ki chhan chhan
tanaffus ki uljhan p tablay ki dhan dhan
y be-ruuh kamron mein khaansi ki than than
sana-khwaan-e taqdiis-e mashriq kahaan hain

y guunje hue qahqahe raaston par
y chaaron taraf bhiir si khirkiyon par

y aavaaze khinchte hue aanchalon par
sana-khwaan-e taqdiis-e mashriq kahaan hain

y phuulon ke gajre y piikon ke chhinte
y bebaak nazrein y gustaakh fiqre
y dhalke badan aur y madquuq chehre
sana-khwaan-e taqdiis-e mashriq kahaan hain

y bhuuki nigaahein hasinon ki jaanib
y badhte hue haath siinon ki jaanib
lapakte hue paanv ziinon ki jaanib
sana-khwaan-e taqdiis-e mashriq kahan hain

yahaan piir bhi aa chuke hain javaan bhi
tanu-mand bete bhi abba miyaan bhi
y biivi bhi hai aur bahan bhi hai maan bhi
sana-khwaan-e taqdiis-e mashriq kahaan hain

maddad chahti hai y havva ki beti
yashodha ki ham-jins raadha ki beti
payambar ki ummat zulekha ki beti
sana-khwaan-e taqdis-e mashriq kahaan hain

zara mulk ke rahbaron ko bulaao
y galiyaan y kuuche y manzar dikhaao
sana-khwaan-e taqdiss-e mashriq ko laao
sana-khwaan-e taqdiis-e mashriq kahan hain

At Noor Jahan's Tomb

Noor Jahan was born in Afghanistan to a noble family of Persian descent. She was married at a young age to the governor of Bihar, who later died in a battle, leaving her with a daughter and few good options. She moved to Agra where she served the royal household as a lady-in-waiting. Historians are not sure whether Emperor Jahangir fell in love with her while she was still married or later when she had moved to Agra. In either case, Jahangir lost no time making Noor Jahan his eighteenth wife. History also shows that it was a very successful marriage and Noor Jahan commanded great political influence as long as she lived.

As a poet, Sahir is not concerned with historical facts. He is using Noor Jahan as a means of drawing attention to the exploitation of women by powerful men for their sexual pleasures. While Noor Jahan may not need our sympathy, countless women are sold into a life of misery with no chance of reclaiming a normal life. We see Sahir once again speaking for oppressed women. When historians write their version of events, it is men's victories and defeats that get the headlines. Women's sufferings get mentioned in the footnotes—if at all.

Alongside the king's tomb,
the resting place of the people's daughter
reminds us of stories
forgotten with the passage of time.
It lifts the veil from a number
of blood-soaked realities,
provides clues about lives
that were crushed.

How, for the comfort of arrogant kings,
beautiful maidens were sold in bazaars,
year after year.
How, for the pleasure of drunken eyes,
youthful bodies were stacked
in red mansions.

How men snatched
half-opened fragrant blossoms
for the adornment of their harems.
How those blossoms were not freed
even when their youth wilted
to maintain the illusion of His Excellency's
romantic aura.

How the slight movement
of one man's lips
doused the lamps of someone's selfless love,
robbed the marital sanctity
of someone's dazzling hands,
shattered cups
filled with the wine of love.

In this scary firmament,
we look at a deserted tomb.
In this silence,
someone is making an urgent appeal.
The wind is howling around cold,
withered branches of trees.
The soul of love
is playing a doleful dirge.

My love, don't look at me
with disbelief
and unfulfilled longing.
None of us can claim to be
either Noor Jahan or Jahangir.
You can move away leaving me,
rejecting me.
My hands are holding your hands.
There is no chain here.

Nuur Jahaan Ke Mazaar Par

pahlu-e shah mein y dukhtar-e jamhuur ki qabr
kitne gum-gashta fasaanon ka pata deti hai
kitne khuun-rez haqaaeq se uthaati hai naqaab
kitni kuchli hui jaanon ka pata deti hai

kaise maghruur shahanshaahon ki taskiin ke liye
saal-haa-saal hasiinaaon ke baazaar lage

Sahir

kaise bahki hui nazron ke ta'ayyush ke liye
surkh mahlon mein javaan jismon ke ambaar lage

kaise har shaakh se munh-band mahakti kaliyaan
noch li jaati thiin taziin-e haram ki khaatir
aur murjha ke kabhi aazaad n ho sakti thiin
zill-e subhaan ki ulfat ke bharam ki khaatir

kaise ik fard ke honton ki zara si jumbish
sard kar sakti thi be-laus vafaaon ke charaagh
luut sakti thi damakte hue haathon ka suhaag
tor sakti thi mai-e i'shq se labrez ayaagh

sahmi sahmi si fazaaon mein y viraan marqad
itna khaamosh hai fariyaad-kunaan ho jaise
sard shaakhon mein hava chiikh rahi hai aise
ruuh-e taqdiis o vafa marsiya-khwaan ho jaise

tu meri jaan mujhe hairat o hasrat se n dekh
ham mein koi bhi jahaan-nuur o jahaan-giir nahien
tu mujhe chhor ke thukra ke bhi ja sakti hai
tere haathon mein mere haath hain zanjiir nahien

Yesterday, Today, Tomorrow

Sahir was a great optimist. Although he was repulsed by what he saw around him—poverty, hunger, degradation—he was convinced that a better dawn was around the corner. The poems in this section cover a wide range of subjects but they carry the same message: our past was problematic, there was bloodshed and carnage, our present is filled with difficult challenges, but our future is bright. The days of our suffering are coming to an end. Living in a secular and democratic society, we can make a difference.

Once Again, the Nook of a Cage

This poem reads like a raw political testament. It is the early 1940s. The Bengal famine is killing thousands each day. War is gaining

130

momentum in Europe, even as India's struggle for freedom is losing
pace. The leaders are divided, weighing different options. The demand
for division of the country is gaining support as never before. There is
an atmosphere of confusion and uncertainty.

For a few moments
there was an outcry,
but then it subsided.
The ancient chain of slavery
was not severed.
Once again,
the flood of adversity
and a snare of waves.
The oarsmen could not decide
what they were supposed
to be doing.

After seeing the breaking
of long-lasting stillness
and its enchantment,
the pulse of hope for the country
rose up but then it drowned.
When it found uncertainty
in the eyes of the leaders,
the dawn drowned
in the shadow of the broken night.

My beloved country!
The gods of your fate
left you under control of strangers.
Because of the demands
of their one-sided politics,
once again, they left you grieving
and mourning.

Once again,
there is a prison of loneliness,

and the same darkness.
Once again,
those old chains
and their murderous jingle.
Once again,
the struggle of man against hunger.
Once again,
the mourning of mothers
and the cries of kids.
Your guides left you for dead.
The plea of Bengal—
give it force
with your drowning voice.

Speak!
Oppressed silence of Chittagong!
Say something.
Speak!
O spring of pus
flowing out of one's chest!
The tempests of hunger
and famine are advancing.
Speak!
The line of funerals of modesty and honour.
Stop those broken steps and ask them.
Pose a question to the long line of skeletons
losing their breath.

How long
will life be shaped
in the cast of oppression?
In these environs,
how long will death swell
and get bigger?

Phir Vohi Kunj-e Qafas

chand lamhon ke liye shor utha duub gaya
kahna zanjiir-e ghulaami ki gir-h kat n saki
phir vohi sail-e bala hai vohi daam-e amvaaj
naa-khudaaon mein safiine ki jagah bat n saki

tuut-te dekh ke deriina taya'attul ka fasuun
nabz-e ummid-e vatan ubhri magar duub gayi
peshvaaon ki nagaahon mein tazabzub pa kar
tuut-ti raat ke saaye mein sahar duub gayi

mere mahbuub vatan! tere muqaddar ke khuda
dast-e aghyaar mein qismat ki i'naan chhor gaye
apni yak-tarfa siyasat ke taqaazon ke tufail
ek baar aur tujhe nauha-kunaan chhor gaye

phir vohi gosha-e zindaan hai vohi taariiki
phir vohi kohna salaasil vohi khuuniin jhankaar
phir vohi bhuuk se insaan ki satiiza-kaari
phir vohi maaon ke nauhe vohi bachchon ki pukaar
tere rahbar tujhe marne ke liye chhor chale
arz-e Bengaal! unhein duubti saanson se pukaar

bol! Chatgaanv ki mazluum khamoshi kuchh bol
bol ai piip se riste hue siinon ki bahaar
bhuuk aur qaht ke tuufaan barhe aate hain
bol ai i'smat-o i'ffat ke janaazon ki qataar!
rok un tuut-te qadmon ko unhein puuchh zara
puuchh ai bhuuk se dam torte dhaanchon ki qataar

zindagi jabr ke saanchon mein dhale gi kab tak
in fazaaon mein abhi maut palegi kab tak

133

Today

This poem lauds the struggle of the working class. It is very similar in tone to 'My Songs are Your Songs', which we read earlier. Towards the end, the poet imagines that foreign rule has ended and the fields are ready to yield a 'crop of gold'. The poet will do what poets have always done: 'I am your songster and for you/whenever I return I will bring new songs.'

Companions!
For several years I wove for you
songs of moons, stars, and springs.
I sang songs of ecstatic love and beauty.
I embellished stately homes of desires.
I was your songster
whenever I came, I came with new songs for you.
But today in the torn hem of my shirt,
there is nothing except the dust of trodden paths.
In the bosom of my harp, my melodies are breathless.
My tunes are lost in the pile of meaningless shouts
and my songs have turned into hiccups.
I'm your songster but not your song
and all the tools I needed to make that song,
my companions,
you have reduced them to ashes.
I'm just holding on to my broken instrument,
while I'm looking at the pile of cold-blooded dead bodies.
All around me, there is a frenzied dance of death
and the animal instincts of men are very much on display.
The apparition of bestiality has arisen
from its dormant state, and with its impure jaws,
it is growling while having its fill of blood.
Kids are frightened though mothers are holding them
in their laps, and the honour of maidens
is very much at stake.
All around there is a commotion

and I stand in this tempest of destruction
getting excited about the fire and blood.
With an empty sack of my songs
I stand totally vanquished
next to paths that are filled
with the debris of broken homes.
I move from door to door
begging for peace and civilized behaviour
hoping that someone will return my songs,
and my tunes to my wounded lips.

Companions!
I sang for you for innumerable years
the songs of revolution and revolt.
In the shadows of the atrocities
of foreign rule, I promoted
the desires of rebellion while waiting to see
the orbit of a new morning in which
the soul of my land is free.
Today, we have broken the chains of servitude
and our country's land and waterways,
roofs and doors, are free from the godforsaken
shadows of foreign rule.
Our fields are ready to give us a crop of gold.
Our valleys are waiting to show their lushness.
In the heart of the mountains, there is an excitement.
Stones and bricks are alive and awake.
In their eyes are hidden the dreams of reconstruction.
Please make their dreams come alive.
Our country's valleys and fields,
women and young girls,
with their open hands are waiting.
Give them the gift of peace and patience
and to the mothers a moment of contentment.
Return to small kids the happiness they lost
for no reason, and free up the country's soul.

Sahir

Return to me the skill and the tunes I once had.
The air is filled with the sounds of 'give me', 'give me'
and in this commotion
I'm going door to door with my sack open
asking for the return of my instruments.
I am your songster and
whenever I return I will bring you new songs.

Aaj

saathio!
main ne barson tumhaare liye
chaand taaron bahaaron ke sapne bune
husn aur i'shq ke giit gaata raha
aarzuon ke aivaan sajaata raha
main tumhaara mughanni tumhaare liye
jab bhi aaya naye giit laata raha
aaj lekin mere daaman-e chaak mein
gard-e raah–e safar ke siva kuchh nahien
mere barbat ke siine mein naghmon ka dam ghut gaya
taanein chiikhon ke ambar mein dab gaii hain
aur giiton ke sur hichkiyaan ban gaye hain
main tumhaara mughanni huun naghma nahien huun
aur naghme ki takhliiq ka saaz o samaan
saathio, aaj tum ne bhasm kar diya hai
aur main apna tuuta hua saaz thaame
sard laashon ke ambar ko tak raha huun
mere chaaron taraf maut ki vahshatein naachti hain
aur insaan ki haivaniyat jaag uthi hai
barbariyat ke khuun khaar i'friit
apne naapaak jabron ko khole
khuun pi pi ke ghurra rahe hain
bachche maaon ki godon mein sahme hue hain
i'smatein sar barahana pareshaan hain
har taraf shor-e aah-o buka hai

aur main is tabaahi ke tuufan mein
aag aur khuun ke haijaan mein
sar niguun aur shikasta makaanon
ke malbe se pur raston par
apne naghmon ki jholi pasaare
dar b dar phir raha huun
mujh ko amn aur tahziib ki bhiik do
miire giiton ki lai mera sur meri nai
mere majruuh honton ko phir saunp do

saathio!
main ne barson tumhaare liye
inqilaab aur baghavat ke naghme aalaape
ajnabi raaj ke zulm ki chhanv mein
sarfroshi ke khwaabida jazbe ubhaare
aur us sub-h ki raah dekhi
jis mein is mulk ki ruuh aazaad ho
aaj zanjiir-e mahkumiyat kat chuki hai
aur is mulk ke bahr o bar baam o dar
ajnabi qaum ke zulmat afshaan pharere ki
manhuus chhanv se aazaad hain
khet sona ugalne ko bechain hain
vaadiyaan lahlahaane ko betaab hain
kohsaaron ke siine mein haijaan hai
sang aur khisht be-khwaab o bedaar hain
un ki aankhon mein taa'miir ke khwaab hain
un ke khwaboon ko takmiil ka ruup do
mulk ki vaadiyaan ghaatiyaan khetiyaan
aurtein bachchiyaan
haath phailaaye khairaat ki muntazir hain
in ko amn aur tahzib ki bhiik do
maaon ko un ke honton ki shaadaabiyaan
nanhe bachchon ko un ki khushi baksh do
mulk ki ruuh ko zindagi bakhsh do
mujh ko mera hunar meri lai bakhsh do

mere sur bakhsh do meri nae bakhsh do
aaj saari faza hai bhikaari
aur main is bhikaari faza mein
apne naghmon ki jholi pasaare
dar ba dar phir raha huun
mujh ko phir mera khoya hua saaz do
main tumhaara mughanni tumhaare liye
jab bhi aaya nae giit laata rahuun ga

What Happened?

India's partition, by all accounts, was a tragedy of epic proportions.
Millions of people perished in the communal bloodshed that followed.
Sahir was passing through Delhi on his way to Lahore at that time,
and therefore he witnessed this tragedy from both sides. This poem,
which was written as a ghazal, portrays sadness at the loss of life and
the suffering caused to the people, but it does not rise to the level of
Amrita Pritam's Waris Shah poem that is mythic in its scope and has a
soul-stirring impact on the reader.

What happened to places
where melodies were once sung
and where idols were worshipped?
O my living heart, what happened
to your departed yearnings?

The land threw up blood
and the sky rained fire.
When some people embraced madness,
what happened to others?

We were worried
about the fate
of their meeting places.
But they agonized
about the lot

of their crazy lovers
whom they had to leave behind.

My failure to believe
was my shortcoming
and so it is today.
But in this state of frenzy,
what happened to those
who kept their faith?

This spectacle
is very hard to recognize.
Ask the razed homes:
what happened
to their bedchambers?

It is good they returned
from the land of non-believers,
safe and unharmed.
But in God's kingdom,
what happened to those
who were burnt and scorched?

Kya Guzri

tarab zaaron p kya biiti sanam khaanon p kya guzri
dil-e zinda tere marhuum armaanon p kya guzri
zamiin ne khuun ugla aasmaan ne aag barsaayi
jab insaanon ke dil badle to insaanon p kya guzri
hamein y fikr un ki anjuman kis haal mein ho gi
unhein y gham k un se chhut ke diivaanon p kya guzri
mera ilhaad to khair ek laa'nat tha so hai ab tak
magar is aa'lam-e vahshat mein iimanon p kya guzri
y manzar kaun sa manzar hai pahchaana nahien jaata
siyaah khaanon se kuchh puuchho shabistaanon p kya guzri
chalo vo kufr ke ghar se salaamat aa gaye lekin
khuda ki mamlikat mein sokhta jaanon p kya guzri

Twenty-sixth January

The twenty-sixth of January is a day of great celebration for Indians everywhere. That was the day when the nation, throwing off the yoke of political slavery, declared itself a sovereign republic. But a revolutionary poet like Sahir, while pleased about certain outcomes, was unhappy about others, especially mass poverty that was still a fact of life. Economic well-being of the masses and the distribution of wealth have always been an important theme for progressive poets. These poets had promised in their verse a better day for all once the fight for independence was over. Sahir was probably writing this poem in the 1960s when the national mood was not at its prime. The Indo-China conflict was a great blow to national pride and faith in our ability to defend ourselves against foreign aggression. Prime Minister Nehru, who once symbolized the hope of new socialist India, died soon after the war. The India–Pakistan War of 1965 was another distraction. There were internal battles being waged within the Congress Party and it took some time for Indira Gandhi to emerge as the leader of one wing of the party. Economic development, which had picked up some speed in the 1950s, faltered, and the issue of poverty surfaced once again.

Sahir starts the poem highlighting the failure of a dream—the dream of abundance for all. Wealth was created but went disproportionately to those who were already wealthy. There was the emergence of a new class of politicians who, forgetting the sacrifices that were made during the freedom struggle by many, focused on enriching themselves. For a country that was deeply religious, religion was of no help. Rather it had turned into a 'disease without any cure'. There were communal and other riots happening everywhere. As a result, 'every street was on fire and every city was a slaughterhouse'. The poet blames everyone including himself for this mess. Reading this poem so many years after Independence, one cannot help but share the poet's concerns. While the country has changed a lot, the fundamental challenge of eradicating poverty remains. The number of people below the poverty line is still high. The rich are growing richer. Religion continues to play a divisive role. And the political leaders are not blameless. We have to ask ourselves: is there any prominent poet who is writing poems like this today?

Let us pause a bit
and reflect on the question:
What happened to the beautiful dreams
that we dreamt?

If wealth increased,
then why is there poverty?
What happened to the plans
of helping the poor?

Those who walked with us
to the gallows,
what happened to those friends,
companions, and lovers?

What price labels are we placing
on the blood of the martyrs?
What happened
to the freedom-lovers we adored?

The naked and helpless
can't afford a coffin.
What happened to the promises
of gold and silver, silk and satin?

I'm asking my democracy-loving friends:
what happened to your
self-proclaimed proclamations?

Why even today
is there no remedy
for a disease called religion?

What happened to those rare
and hard-to-find prescriptions?

Every street is on fire
and every city is a slaughterhouse.
What happened
to the ideals of oneness of mankind?

Life is aimlessly wandering
in the deserts of darkness.
What happened to the moons
that appeared in the sky?

If I'm the culprit,
you're a sinner too.
And leaders of the nation,
you too are not blameless.

Chhabiis Janvari

aao k aaj ghour karein is savaal par
dekhe the ham ne jo voh hasiin khwaab kya huye
daulat barhi to mulk mein aflaas kyun barha
khush haali-e avaam ke asbaab kya huye
jo apne saath saath chale ku-e daar tak
vo dost vo rafiiq vo ahbaab kya huye
kya mol lag raha hai shahidon ke khuun ka
marte the jin p ham vo saza-yaab kya huye
be kas barahnagi ko kafan tak nahien nasiib
voh va'da haa-e atlas o kim khwaab kya huye
jamhuriyat navaaz bashar dost aman khwaah
khud ko jo khud diye the voh alqaab kya hue
mazhab ka rog aaj bhi kyun la-ilaaj hai
voh nuskha haaye naadar o naayaab kya huye
har kuucha sho'la zaar hai har shahr qatl gaah
yak jahti-e hayaat ke aadaab kya huye

sahra-e tiirgi mein bhatakti hai zindagi
ubhre the jo ufuq p voh mahtaab kya huye
mujrim huun main agar to gunahgaar tum bhi ho
ai rahbaraan-e qaum khata-kaar tum bhi ho

Let Us Weave a Dream

This is a forward-looking poem, filled with an abundance of positive emotions. Poets have always referred to themselves as dream merchants. They see the future differently from most other folks. Sahir admits at the start that he has lived his life with the help of his dreams, namely, of the beloved's charms, of achieving greater mastery over his craft, of making his country a better place. And the death of these dreams, whenever it happened, was catastrophic. That is why dreaming about our tomorrow, about our future, is such an important task. The words of this poem slowly sink in and they bring richness and hope into our lives.

Let us weave a dream
for our tomorrow
with the intent of preventing
this night of today's arduous time
from poisoning our body and soul—
disabling it
from weaving another dream.

Although this life of mine
has been running
on the fast track,
I have lived it
with the help of my dreams.

Dreaming of my beloved's tresses,
her lips and her body.
Dreaming of achieving
the heights of artistry
and mastery of the craft

of versification.
Dreaming of the art of
civilized living
and the country's well-being.
Dreaming of the prisons
and paths
that lead to places
where bodies are hung.

These dreams
were assets of my youth;
these dreams were the foundation
of whatever I did.
When these dreams died,
my life lost its colourful trappings.
It feels that 'my life's hand
has been placed
under the weight
that it can't bear'.[15]

Let us weave
a dream for our tomorrow
with the intent of preventing
this night of today's arduous time
from poisoning our body and soul—
disabling it from weaving
another dream.

Aao Ke Koi Khwaab Bunein

aao k koi khwaab bunein kal ke vaaste
varna y raat aaj ke sangiin daur ki

---

[15] This metaphor of a 'hand under the weight of a stone' originally comes
from Mirza Ghalib but it was very effectively used by Faiz Ahmed Faiz, who
titled one of his poetry collections using this metaphor.

das legi jaan o dil ko kuchh aaise k jaan o dil
taa u'mr phir n koi hasiin khwaab bun sakein

go ham se bhaagti rahi hai y tez gaam u'mr
khwaabon ke aasre p kaati hai tamam u'mr

zulfon ke khwaab honton ke khwaab aur badan ke khwaab
me'raaj-e fan ke khwaab kamaal-e sukhan ke khwaab
tahziib-e zindagi ke farogh-e vatan ke khwaab
zindaan ke khwaab kuucha-e daar o rasan ke khwaab

y khwaab hi to apni javaani ke paas the
y khwaab hi to apne amal ki asaas the
y khwaab mar gaye hain to berang hai hayaat
yuun hai k jaise 'dast-e tah-e sang' hai hayaat

aao k koi khwaab bunein kal ke vaaste
varna y raat aaj ke sangiin daur ki
das legi jaan o dil ko kuchh aaise k jaan o dil
taa u'mr phir n koi hasiin khwaab bun sakein

Neither a Hindu Nor a Muslim

As a staunch secularist, Sahir was always wary of the role that religion plays in society. While all religions teach love and tolerance, in practice, religion is a tool in the hands of people who like to create divisions and profit from them. This poem is actually a lyric written for the film *Dhuul Ka Phuul* (1959) and sung by Mohammad Rafi in his inimitable voice; it gained immense popularity. There is no better song than this one to promote the great ideal of secularism.

You're neither a Hindu nor a Muslim.
You are a descendant of humans;
you will grow up to be a human being.

It's good that you have no name yet;
and you have nothing to do with any religion.

The knowledge that has divided humans;
you don't share any blame in that.

You will become the emblem of changing times.
You are a descendant of humans;
you will grow up to be a human being.

God created us with just human attributes;
but we labelled ourselves as Hindus and Muslims.
Nature bequeathed us one common land;
but we created India here and Iran there.

You will become the storm that breaks all barriers.
You are a descendant of humans;
you will grow up to be a human being.

You do not own the faith that teaches hate.
The foot that suppresses another is not yours.
The temple that does not embrace the Quran is not yours;
The mosque that does not encompass the Gita is not yours.

You will become the yearning for peace and friendship.
You are a descendant of humans;
you will grow up to be a human being.

Tu Hindu Banega ...

tu Hindu bane ga n Musalmaan bane ga
insaan ki aulaad hai insaan bane ga

achha hai abhi tak tera kuchh naam nahien hai
tujh ko kisi mazhab se koi kaam nahien hai
jis i'lm ne insaanon ko taqsiim kiya hai
us i'lm ka tujh par koi ilzaam nahien hai

tu badle hue vaqat ki pehchaan bane ga
insaan ki aulaad hai insaan bane ga

maalik ne har insaan ko insaan banaya
ham ne use Hindu ya Musalmaan banaaya
qudrat ne to bakhshi thi hamein ek hi dharti
ham ne kahiin Bhaarat kahiin Iraan banaya

jo tor de har bandh voh tuufaan bane ga
insaan ki aulaad hai insaan bane ga

nafrat jo sikhaaye vo dharam tera nahien hai
insaan ko jo raunde voh qadam tera nahien hai
Quraan n ho jis mein voh mandir nahien tera
Giita n ho jis mein voh haram tera nahien hai

tu amn ka aur sul-ha ka armaan bane ga
insaan ki aulaad hai insaan bane ga

The Pathfinders

Sahir was greatly inspired by the poetry of Allama Iqbal, though he differed with him strongly on his religious worldview. Iqbal in Sahir's eyes was a pathfinder (pioneer, groundbreaker, or a trailblazer). Sahir also showed great admiration for some of his contemporaries, especially Faiz Ahmed Faiz. In this section we have poems about three people he admired. One thing that the reader will notice is that in all these cases Sahir's poetic work goes beyond the profile of the person he was writing about: for example, ideals do not die with the leader (Nehru); you can't honour the poet without honouring the language in which the poet wrote his work (Ghalib); and time sometimes completely changes the legacy of a leader (Lenin).

Jawaharlal Nehru

Sahir started his life as a committed Leftist or communist while India was still under foreign rule. His poetry right from the beginning reflected his anti-capitalist bias. But after Independence it was clear that the Communist Party of India was politically too weak to establish a government at the national level. On the other hand, the Congress Party under Prime Minister Nehru's leadership had chosen socialism as an ideal for India's economic development. Nehru was also playing a role at the international level that was pro-Soviet and anti-American in many respects. In view of this, Sahir felt that Congress was more likely to deliver on promises, like land reforms, trade union rights, pro-public sector industrial policy, than the Communist Party.

Unlike many of his progressive colleagues, Sahir was never affiliated with the Communist Party as a member. Therefore, it was easy for him to switch his loyalty. Sahir became a great admirer of Nehru as he saw in him someone who could deliver for the masses what poets like him had been advocating. When Nehru passed away, Sahir felt the loss at a personal level. This poem is unique in many respects. First, every line of the poem is written with utmost sincerity. Second, it starts as a philosophical meditation on the nature of death; not about what death can do but what death cannot do. Third, it lists Nehru's achievements as a leader with great beauty. Many poems were written about Nehru on his demise but this one stands out for its poetic quality as well the emotional intensity.

When physical form disappears,
it is not the end of our being.
When we lose our flesh and bones,
we aren't completely effaced.
When the heart stops beating,
it is not the death of our aspirations.
When breathing climaxes,
it is not the end of our proclamations.
When lips freeze,
it is not the end of our affirmations.
When physical form disappears,
it is not the end of our being.

He stayed away from all faiths,
yet he was the fraternizer of all faiths.

Carrying the burden of the sins of all nations,
he walked, all his life, carrying the cross
like Jesus.

He suffered the consequences
of peoples' decision to divide,
but he never lost faith
in the brotherhood of all humans.

In his eyes,
he nurtured a dream
of global civilization.
Every breath that he took signalled
the dawn of a new era.

Not tolerating inequities
of the capitalist system,
he stayed committed
to the constitution of equality.

Honour his affirmations
and his proclamations.
We divided his ashes;
let's equally share his longings
and yearnings too.

Standing at the confluence
of life and death,
why are we perplexed?
Just carry the tricoloured banner
that he bequeathed.

The one who informs us
of our path to our journey's end,
let us walk with the imprint
of those footsteps on our forehead.

On the edges of time,
we shouldn't have stains of blood.
In search of one clear centre,
let us walk there with our temples
and mosques.

We shall overcome tensions
between capital and labour
if we walk with conviction
and determination.

He was confident
of our present and our future,
let us walk carrying the rapture of his dreams
and his soul's despairs.

When physical form disappears,
it is not the end of our being.
When we lose our flesh and bones,
we aren't completely effaced.
When the heart stops beating,
it is not the death of our aspirations.
When breathing climaxes,
it is not the end of our proclamations.
When lips freeze,
it is not the end of our affirmations.

Jawaharlal Nehru

jism ki maut koi maut nahien hoti hai
jism mit jaane se insaan nahien mar jaate
dharkanein rukne se armaan nahien mar jaate
saans tham jaane se a'laan nahien mar jaate
hont jam jaane se farmaan nahien mar jaate
jism ki maut koi maut nahien hoti hai

voh jo har diin se munkar tha har ik dharam se duur
phir bhi har diin har ik dharam ka gham khwaar raha

saari quomon ke gunaahon ka kara bojh liye
u'mr bhar suurat-e iisa jo sar-e daar raha

jis ne insaanon ki taqsiim ke sadme jhaile
phir bhi insaan ki akhvat ka parastaar raha

jis ki nazron mein tha ik aa'lmi tahziib ka khwaab
jis ka har saans naye a'hd ka m'maar raha

jis ne zardaar mashiiat ko gavaara n kiya
jis ko aaiine musavaat p israar raha

us ke farmaanon ki a'ilaanon ki taaziim karo
raakh taqsiim ki armaan bhi taqsiim karo

maut aur ziist ke sangam pe pareshaan kyun ho
us ka bakhsha hua seh rang-e alam le ke chalo

jo tumhein jaadha-e manzil ka pata deta hai
apni peshaani p naqshe qadam le ke chalo

daaman-e vaqt p ab khuun ke chhiinte na parein
ek markaz ki taraf dair o haram le ke chalo

ham mita daalein ge sarmaaya o mehnat ka tazaad
y aqiida y iraada y qasam le ke chalo

vo jo hamraaz raha haazr o mustaqabil ka
us ke khwaabon ki khushi ruuh ka gham le ke chalo

jism ki maut koi maut nahien hoti hai
jism mit jaane se insaan nahien mar jaate
dharkanein rukne se armaan nahien mar jaate

saans tham jaane se a'laan nahien mar jaate
hont jam jaane se farmaan nahien mar jaate

A Celebration of Ghalib

It is an interesting attribute of India's political culture that leaders from time to time discover a forgotten national figure—a poet, a philosopher, a religious leader—and all kinds of celebrations are staged with great deal of fanfare in memory of that person. Once the celebrations are over, it is business as usual. In 1969, it was the death centenary of Urdu's greatest poet, Mirza Ghalib. *'Jashn-e Ghalib'* was written by Sahir in February 1969. A poet who was almost forgotten suddenly became the subject of exhibitions, national symposia, publications, etc. Sahir was an admirer of Ghalib's poetry, but what he is objecting to here is the exhibitionism of public personalities, the hypocrisy of paying tribute to Urdu's greatest poet while the language in which he wrote was being called the language of treason and being systematically excluded from public discourse and the country's education system.

Twenty-one years passed
after our complete freedom
and then we thought of Ghalib.
Where is he buried?
Where did he live?
Our poetry-loving minds
raised these questions.

The grave
that craved a cover
for one hundred years
now has flowers of devotion
as an act of our showmanship.
To say that it is about Urdu
does not solve the mystery.
This tumultuous celebration—
is it a service or a conspiracy?

In the cities
where the melodies of Ghalib
were once heard,
in those places
Urdu has no name, no recognition.
The day we won our independence
this language was labelled
the language of curse and treachery.

The political system
that killed this living language,
why is that system disheartened
by the departed?
The poet named Ghalib
was a poet of Urdu.
Why oppress the language
and be kind to Ghalib?

These riotous celebrations
are interesting tools of trade.
This is the effort of a few
to make some others feel good.
Those who could not be satisfied
with false promises
would probably feel good
with this festivity.

Greetings for this jubilation!
But let us face the truth.
We as people are unable
to face the reality.
It is either Gandhi or Ghalib;
in the eyes of justice
we are killers of both,
we are devotees of both.

Sahir

Jashn-e Ghalib

ikkiis baras guzre aazaadi-e kaamil ko
tab ja ke kahiin ham ko ghalib ka khayaal aaya
turbat hai kahaan us ki maskan tha kahan us ka
ab apne sukhan-parvar zehnon mein savaal aaya

sau saal se jo turbat chaadar ko tarasti thi
ab us p aqiidat ke phuulon ki numaaish hai
urdu ke ta'lluq se kuchh bhed nahien khulta
y jashn y hangaama khidmat hai k saazish hai

jin shahron mein guunji thi ghalib ki nava barson
un shahron mein ab urdu benaam o nishaan thahri
aazaadi-e kaamil ka e'laan hua jis din
maa'tuub zabaan thahri gaddaar zabaan thahri

jis a'hd-e siyaasat ne y zinda zabaan kuchli
us a'hd-e siyaasat ko marhuum ka gham kyon hai
ghalib jise kahte hain urdu hi ka shaa'yir tha
urdu p sitem dha kar ghalib p karam kyun hai

y jashn y hangaame dilchasp khilaune hain
kuchh logon ki koshish hai kuchh log bahal jaayein
jo va'da-e farda par ab tal nahien sakte hain
mumkin hai ki kuchh arsa is jashn p tal jaayein

y jashn mubarak ho par y bhi sadaqat hai
ham log haqiiqat ke ehsaas se aari hain
gaandhi ho k ghalib ho insaaf ki nazron mein
ham donon ke qaatil hain donon ke pujaari hain

On Lenin's 100th Birthday

This ghazal-poem was written in April 1970 to mark Lenin's birth centenary. By the early 1970s, the communist movement had seen major fissures. The Soviet Union and China had parted ways. Mao's cultural revolution was aimed at consolidating his own power base. The Soviet regime had admitted to gross human rights violations and the killing of millions under Stalin's rule. Independent reporting showed that Lenin was no different from Stalin in terms of the brutalities he committed against his own people. These revelations were disturbing for progressives because they had always looked upon the Soviet Union as a workers' paradise where their rights were protected, unlike in capitalist societies. Those who believed in the infallibility of the unified communist doctrine were puzzled and disappointed. They were trying to adjust to the new situation.

This ghazal is Sahir's attempt to come to terms with the new reality. He bemoans the fact that there were now more preachers (political theorists) with more interpretations and as a result the crux of the message was being altered. The last couplet is significant. Workers and farmers were divided in their struggles against the capitalist regimes before the advent of Marxist ideology. The idea of a socialist revolution unified them. But now there were divisions, and these divisions were doing great damage to the movement.

Confused, I don't know
where the followers are going.
But the number of your preachers
is getting bigger and bigger.

In the West and the East
the interpretations of your message,
O messenger, are being altered.

The people who until yesterday
talked of friendship,
are degrading the honour and dignity
of their own folks.

The politics of the new age
has a different look and feel.

The new ruling systems
are running out of steam.

We came from different classes
but are now divided into factions.
The slaves might run out of their luck
before it is time.

Kya Jaanein Teri Ummat

kya jaanein teri ummat kis haal ko pahunche gi
bharti chali jaati hai taadaad imaamon ki
har gosha-e maghrib mein har khitta-e mashriq mein
tashriih digar guun hai ab tere payaamon ki
voh log jinhein kal tak daava tha rifaaqat ka
tazliil p utre hain apnon hi ke namon ki
bigre hue tevar hain nau-u'mr siyaasat ke
biphri hui saansein hain nau-mashq nizaamon ki
tabqon se nikal kar ham firqon mein n bat jaaein
ban kar n bigar jaae taqdiir ghulaamon ki

2
Poems
War and Peace

If we failed to raise our voice
then this dazzling mound of dust
shall not be safe again.
Our land will not be safe,
our sky will not be safe
from the evil spirits brought to life
by the madness of atom.

—'The Shadows'

Good neighbours need to live peacefully. This holds even more true for nations that share common history and culture. Unfortunately, India and Pakistan have a history of wars and conflicts that have been particularly fraught. 'O Noble Souls' was broadcast in 1967, on the first anniversary of the Tashkent Agreement, which laid a path to peace between these two countries. The 1965 war had been a rude awakening for poets and intellectuals, who thought that such a thing could never happen. But unfortunately this agreement did not bring about lasting peace, as Bangladesh's struggle for freedom once again brought these two countries to the theatre of war.

O Noble Souls

The poem is written from a leftist perspective, but its main arguments have stood the test of time. In the first part, the poet argues that war itself is a problem, so how can it be a solution for anything? The second part of the poem is 'pro-war'—a war against poverty and hunger and the inequities of the capitalist system, one that is far from over: Farmers in several parts of the country still struggle for decent livelihood. Schools, especially in rural areas, are poorly equipped. In spite of massive progress on several fronts, much remains to be accomplished. Economic development, especially in urban areas, has brought forth new challenges, such as pollution, that are hazardous and need to be addressed. Therefore, to paraphrase the poet, there is enough to fight for the good of the people and that should remain the focus at all times.

1

Blood,
our own or someone else's,
after all
is the blood of human beings.
War,
whether in the East or in the West,
is slaughter
of world peace.

Bombs are dropped
over homes or at the border—
their wounds leave a mark
on the soul for a long time.
Fields burn, our own
or those of others—
life is vexed by want and hunger.
Tanks move forward
or they retreat—
Earth's womb goes barren.
Whether celebration of victory
or defeat's mourning—
Life cries
at funeral processions.

War itself is a problem.
How can it provide
a solution for anything?

Its gift today is fire and blood.
And tomorrow
it will bring hunger,
want, and scarcity.

That is why,
O Noble Souls,
if war is postponed,
it is all for the good.
If the candles continue to burn
in your and our courtyards,
it is all for the good.

2

To show
that you are better than others—
is it essential to spill blood?
To end the darkness of your hearth,
is it essential to burn homes?

There are other wars we need to fight.
Don't limit it to the fields of blood
and slaughter.
Reason could be life's purpose;
do not limit it
to the pursuit of madness alone.

Let us come together
in this unfortunate world
to spread the light of thought
and imagination.
The things that empower world peace,
let us plan those efforts
and endeavours.

A war to eradicate fear
and barbarism;
We need peace
for evolving our civilization.
A war to end the politics of killing;
We need peace for human comfort
and security.

A war to fight poverty
and slavery.
We need peace
for a better system.
A war to stop leaders
who have lost their way.
We need peace
for the well-being of hapless people.

A war to correct
the capitalist system's inequities.
We need peace
for the happiness of the masses.
A war to eliminate the thinking
that produces it.
We need peace
for a peaceful life.

Ai Sharif Insaano

1

khuun apna ho ya paraya ho
nasl-e aadam ka khuun hai aakhir
jang mashriq mein ho k maghrib mein
amn-e aa'lam ka khuun hai aakhir

bam gharon par girein k sarhad par
ruuh-e taa'miir zakhm khaati hai

khet apne jalein k auron ke
ziist faaqon se tilmalaati hai
tank aage barhein k piichhe hatein
kokh dharti ki baanjh hoti hai
fat-h ka jashn ho k haar ka sog
zindagi mayyaton p roti hai

jang to khud hi ek mas-ala hai
jang kya masa-lon ka hal degi
aag aur khuun aaj bakhshe gi
bhuuk aur ehtiyaaj kal degi

is liye ai sharif insano!
jang talti rahe to behtar hai
aap aur ham sabhi ke aangan mein
sham'a jalti rahe to behtar hai

2

bartari ke subuut ki khaatir
khuun bahaana hi kya zaruuri hai
ghar ki taarikiyaan mitaane ko
ghar jalana hi kya zaruuri hai

jang ke aur bhi to maidaan hain
sirf maidaan-e kisht o khuun hi nahien
haasil-e zindagi khirad bhi hai
haasil-e zindagi junuun hi nahien

aao is tiira-bakht duniya mein
fikr ki raushni ko aam karein
amn ko jin se taqviyat pahunche
aisi jangon ka ehtmaam karein

jang vahshat se barbriyat se
amn tahziib o irtiqa ke liya

jang marg-aafriin siyaasat se
amn insaan ki baqa ke liye

jang iflaas aur ghulaami se
amn behtar nizaam ki khaatir
jang bhatki hui qayaadat se
amn be-bas a'vaam ki khaatir

jang sarmaaye ke tasallut se
amn jamhuur ki khushi ke liye
jang jangon ke falsafe ke khilaaf
amn pur-amn zindagi ke liye

The Shadows

'The Shadows', 'Parchhaaiyaan' in Urdu, was brought out as a booklet
by a publishing company based in Lahore in 1955. Sahir wrote in the
foreword:

> Parchhaaiyaan is my first long poem. This poem is part of the
> movement which is under way to safeguard peace and civilization. I
> feel that it is the responsibility of each new generation to protect the
> land that it inherits from its ancestors. They should aspire to make their
> inheritance better and even more beautiful. My poem is the literary
> face of this endeavour.[1]

Ali Sardar Jafri, who wrote the preface to 'Parchhaaiyaan', had this
to say:

> The poem is important for two reasons. First, it deals with a most
> important issue which concerns all humanity. The global peace
> movement is based on the premise that it is affirmed by every country,
> every nation, every ethnicity, every race and class, and every thoughtful
> individual. Nearly half of the world's population has stamped their

[1] Sahir Ludhianvi, *Parchchaaiyaan* (Lahore: Maktaba Jadeed, 1955), 6–7.

commitment for world peace. By writing this poem, Sahir Ludhianvi has put his signature in support of this movement. The second reason is that Sahir has presented his thesis in the form of a story, which simplifies an otherwise complex situation. Many of our best poems fail to make an impact because they stay above the level of comprehension of the ordinary reader. But Sahir's *Parchhaaiyaan* because of its simple story and uncomplicated poetic narration will reach a large number of people. More than 90% words used are part of our day-to-day conversation. Sahir didn't unduly burden his work in the name of tradition or classicism. His success arises from the directness of his expression aimed at capturing the harsh realities of our time ... The poetic technique used is also new and has not been employed by any other Urdu poet. The more I think about it the more I come to the conclusion that Sahir's association with films as a lyricist had much to do with it. There is a visual dimension that only a poet familiar with film photography could bring to the poem.[2]

Sajjad Zaheer, who is one of the founding fathers of the Progressive Writers' Movement, heard Sahir recite 'Parchhaaiyaan' in a poetical gathering. He wrote:

I heard Sahir's poem in a mushaira. I was surprised because a typical mushaira is a place for reciting ghazals that are simple and appeal to the masses. Sahir took a bold step. It was a very cold night and late into the evening. It was a point in the mushaira when people start to think about going home. But no one left. Sahir had recited only the first stanza of the poem when I felt that he was slowly transporting us to a magical world. He was sharing with us the frustrations of two lovers whose innocent lives were caught up in a global conflict.... At that time, I realized that Sahir, through the medium of his poem, had reached the highest and the most sacred heights of the art of writing poetry. The poet was giving voice to millions of countrymen who wanted to live in peace. This poem contains delightfulness and wizardry that is pure Indian. Think of a flower-laden bush of *champa* whose fragrance engulfs us during the heat of the rainy season. But

---

[2] Ludhianvi, *Parchchaaiyaan*, 9–11.

alongside it has universal appeal too. This fragrance travels far and wide, much beyond the boundaries of the garden where the bush was located and where this aroma was born.[3]

'*Parchhaaiyaan*' is incomparable in terms of the intensity of its anti-war message. Sahir is laser-focused on his central idea, namely, the preservation of global peace. The horrors of the preparation for war are portrayed alongside the unravelling lives of two ordinary lovers caught up in this whirlwind of war. The poet leaves the reader wondering whether this is an account of something that actually happened, or what could happen in the future if we are not careful. A reader familiar with 20th-century English literature is reminded of a famous poem by T.S. Eliot titled 'The Waste Land', a long poem published in 1922, when the horrors of the First World War were still fresh in the minds of all Europeans. Eliot's poem is divided into five sections that depict disillusionment and despair, role playing by some characters, death and self-denial, lyrical petition, and an image of a judgement. If you read these two poems one after the other, you will be struck by some common themes and imagery that run in quick succession, like a slideshow. 'The Waste Land' ends with a Sanskrit mantra—'*Shantih, Shantih, Shantih*'—to reveal its hidden meaning. Sahir, however, does not indulge in religious or ethical reasoning. He follows a simple 'if–then' logic: If there is another war, not only will homes be destroyed and lives lost, there will be such devastation that those who survive would carry no memories and no moments of solitude.

The scenario presented in the poem—a global war, conscription of Indian soldiers to fight someone else's battle, a foreign power's control over war and peace-making, etc.—makes it clear that it was written not in 1955, as is generally understood, but around 1944 or 1945, when Sahir lived in Lahore. According to one account, this poem was first published in an Urdu magazine called *Chattaan*, edited by Shorish Kashmiri, one of Sahir's close friends. The poem, whenever

---

[3] Sajjad Zaheer, '*Phuulon Se Ladi Hui Champa Ki Khushbu*', *Fan aur Shakhsiyat*, 17–18, 1985: 341–2.

written, whenever published, will always be remembered as unique in
Urdu literature.

Writing a war poem, especially highlighting its destructive impact
on society as a whole, was a favourite topic among the progressive poets.
But a poem that mirrored the horrors of war against the backdrop
of a relationship between two individuals—perhaps a romantic
relationship—and how it impacted those lives was something different
and special. Only two progressive poets—Sahir and Faiz—were able to
bring together the really big and the really small successfully. Whether
it was about revolution or war, a poet like Josh Malihabadi came
across noisily, unloading a whole carriage of slogans and affirmations,
while Sahir and Faiz made a deep connection with the inner chords of
being, through a velvet romantic softness and mysteriously captivating
meaning-making. Another noteworthy factor where both these poets
distinguished themselves was musicality; the rhythmical flow of
words and movements that introduced tonal variations turned their
poems into musical compositions: a lament for the dead, or perhaps a
covenant or disposition for the living.

In the heart of the adolescent night,
there is a milky edge
that is fidgeting like a dream
made of shiny marble.
Beautiful flowers, beautiful leaves,
beautiful branches
are flexibly bending down
like a maiden's body.
The soft contours of the horizon
have blended into the air.
The land spouts loveliness
as if it were the land of our dreams.
Shadows arise in my imagination.
Sometime as guesses,
other times as certainties.
The trees, under whose shadows

we sought protection,
are standing motionless
like a trusted guardian.

Under those very trees today,
once again, two living hearts
have come to say something
and to listen to the words
with their silent lips.
I don't know with how much struggle
and how much effort
they have succeeded to come here,
by stealing moments
that have the feel of being partially asleep
and partially awake.

This is how we felt the air,
it was the same season,
the same years—
that is where the journey
of our love commenced.
With fast-throbbing hearts
and wishful eyes we offered
our little prayers
for lotus buds to become big flowers.
We wished for the acceptance
of prayers that came from
deep within us.
Shadows arise in my imagination.

You are coming to meet me,
hiding from the eyes of the people around,
with downcast eyes
and body as if it were a stolen object.
You were afraid of the sound
of your own footsteps,

and the movement of your own shadow.
Shadows arise in my imagination.

A little boat is moving
with the force of the wind.
The boatman sings a song
matching the sound of the flowing water.
Your body shakes
when the wave hits
and you fall into my arms.
Shadows arise in my imagination.

I am pinning a flower in your combed hair.
Your eyes lower themselves with joy.
God knows what I am going to say today!
My tongue is dry
and my voice is rapidly wearing down.
Shadows arise in my imagination.

You have wrapped
your delicate arms around my neck.
The shadow of my smile
is falling on your lips.
I am certain
that nothing would separate us now.
You are concerned
that we are separate even in this union.
Shadows arise in my imagination.

You are arranging my books
randomly spread on the bed
with great reverence.
You are singing those songs in tender tones
that are sung on the wedding night
by women to the accompaniment of drums.
Shadows arise in my imagination.

How heart-warming were those moments,
and how lovely were those points in time.
How delicate were those decorations
worn by the grooms,
how attractive were those pearl strings.
Every small alley of our village
was filled with greenery,
making the place look like an island of dreams.
Each breath we took
and each wave of the morning breeze
felt like a melody.

Suddenly the sound of booted footsteps
was heard from the other side of the fields
whose green shoots were dancing wildly in the wind.
The breeze coming from the west
had the smell of gunpowder.
On the bright face of construction
the cloud of destruction spread widely.
The dance of savageness was seen in each village,
and the wilderness of the forest spread into cities.
From the civilized countries of the west
came some uniformed officers—
boasting, cheering, and swaying.
Ropes of tents were thrust
into the heart of the silent fields.
Soft paths were scarred
from people walking wearing heavy boots.
The horrifying military bands
overwhelmed the delicate sound
of the spinning wheel.
The fiery dust raised by the passing jeeps
drowned the apparel of flowers.

Human beings became cheap,
produce became expensive.

Traditional meeting places got empty,
the lines in front of recruiting offices
became longer and longer.
The graceful and bright youth of the village
left after they were recruited as soldiers.
The paths that did not return many
became well worn.
The friends who left
lost their conscience and their adolescence.
Mothers' grown-up sons
and sisters' adorable brothers—
they all left.

The village was gripped by sadness,
the spring that usually came with the festivals
disappeared.
The swings tied to the delicate branches
of mango trees vanished too.
Bazaars were covered with dust,
and hunger started to sprout in the fields.
Everything of value
flew from the shops
into underground storage.
The plight of distressed homes
increased to troubling levels.
The rise in prices brought famine.
The shepherds lost their way,
water maidens left their water holes.
Weak and helpless virgins
left their parents' homes.

Poverty-stricken peasants
sold their implements, their bullocks,
and their fields.
The desire to survive drove them
to sell the means

by which they could have made a living.
When nothing was left to sell
then the flesh trade started.
What was not allowed in private
was now encouraged in crowded places.
Shadows arise in my imagination.

You are coming with your head bare,
your hair tousled,
carrying the burden
of thousands of accusations,
stripped naked by lustful eyes,
trying to cover your body's nakedness.
Shadows arise in my imagination.

I have been to the city
looking at several possibilities.
No one valued what I had to offer.
From the gambling places
of the political oppressors,
there was no fair offer
for the skills I had to offer.
Shadows arise in my imagination.

In your home there is clamour
of the Day of Judgement.
The mailman has brought a telegram
from the front.
The one who was dearer to you
than your own life,
that brother has perished
in the 'enemy's hell'.
Shadows arise in my imagination.

Every step of the way
there is a crowd of ill fame.

Every bend in the way
opens doors to infamy.
There is no friendship, no courtesy,
no loveliness, no sincerity.
No one belongs to anyone.
Everyone seems to be a loner.
Shadows arise in my imagination.

I don't know this pathway
that is deserted like my heart
is going to take you anywhere.
You are being slain
by the killers of ethics and morality.
The redness seen in the horizon
is coming from the bleeding
of my heart's desires.
Shadows arise in my imagination.

I remember the evening
wrapped in the sun's blood.
I remember how the glowing dreams of love
came to an end.
That evening reminded me
that in this world
the smile of maidens
is traded the same way
as a farmer's field.
That evening reminded me
how in the capitalist system
the relationship between two innocent souls
is also put up for sale.

That evening I came to know
that when a father's assets are sold,
a mother's gleaming dreams
go up for sale too.

That evening I came to know
that when the brother is killed in a war
then the sister's youth is traded
in rich men's pleasure houses.
I remember the evening
wrapped in the sun's blood.
I remember how the glowing dreams of love
came to an end.

Today, while sitting alone
or being an object of desire in an assembly
several thousand miles away from me,
you are weaving dreams of me
sitting in someone's lap.

And I work very hard day and night
carrying love's agony in my heart.
I die for the sake of living.
I make fun of my talent
while making a stranger feel good.

I am helpless.
You are helpless.
Helpless is this whole world.
My inner pain
is weighing on my mind.
The price of living
is either the gallows or disgrace.

I could not get to the stakes
and you could not get
to the end of your struggle.
You could not embrace
what you wanted.
We are two souls
that have failed to reach
their goals.

We are living with pyres
flaming out from our breaths.
Our commitments burn silently.
For those afflicted by the realities of life,
even the garbs of their dreams are burning.
I see two shadows lurking
in the midst of trees once where we met.
Once again two hearts have come forward
to mingle and to blend.
Once again I see the hurricane of death rising,
the clouds of war appearing.

I am wondering
whether these two would meet
the same end as ours.
Their passion too would be defamed.
Who knows whether their future
also holds a blood-soaked evening.

I remember the evening
wrapped in the sun's blood.
I remember how the glowing dreams of love
came to an end.

Our love could not stand against
the forces of misfortune,
but I wish these two will achieve
the night of their deeply held desires.
We were given the task of dying endlessly,
but we wish these two lovers the melodious
and playful gift of life.

For a long time now
the game of politics is played this way:
kids get killed
when they grow up.

For a long time now
rulers have been obsessed
with sowing the seeds of famine
in faraway lands.

For a long time now
the dreams of youth are treated
like a wasteland.
For a long time now
love has been frantically searching
for a place of its own.
For a long time now
the beauty of life
is looking for ways
to save its honour
walking oppressive trails.

Let us address
all those devastated souls
that they should give their wounds
a voice and let them speak.
Our secret is no longer strictly ours.
It is shared by all.
Let us include the whole world
as partner in this mystery.

Let us rise up
and tell the political players
that we hate these games of war.
If the apparel of life
comes only in the colour of blood
then we don't want it.

Let us say
clearly and loudly
that if any assassin came our way
then with every step approaching

the ground underneath
would shrink.
Each wave of breeze
will change its direction,
and every branch
will take the colour of stones.

Let us rise
and tell every warmonger
that we need implements
to do our work.
We do not wish to possess
anyone else's land,
but we need ploughs
for tilling the land that we own.

Let us say
that we do not want to see a trader
come our way.
We are not going to put up
any more virgins for sale.
Our fields have woken up,
our crops are standing upright.
In this place,
we are not going to sell
even a small patch of land.
This land is the land of
Gautam and Nanak.
On this sacred soil
no savages would be allowed
to walk again.
Our blood is held in trust
for the new generation.
No garrisons will feed
on our blood once again.

If we failed to raise our voice
then this dazzling mound of dust
shall not be safe again.
Our land will not be safe,
our sky will not be safe
from the evil spirits brought to life
by the madness of atom.

During the last war
our homes were burnt,
but this time
don't be surprised
if our moments of solitude
are burnt, too.
During the last war
forms and figures were burnt
but this time
don't be surprised
if our shadows are burnt, too.

Shadows arise in my imagination.

Parchhaaiyaan

javaan raat ke siine p duudhia aanchal
machal raha hai kisi khwaab-e marmariin ki tarah
hasiin phuul hasein pattiyaan hasein shaakhein
lachak rahi hain kisi jism-e nazniin ki tarah
faza mein ghul se gaye hain ufaq ke narm khatuut
zamiin hasiin hai khwaabon ki sarzamiin ki tarah

tassuvaraat ki parchhaaiyaan ubharti hain
kabhi gumaan ki surat kabhi yaqiin ki tarah
voh per jin ke tale ham panaah lete the
khare hain aaj bhi saakat kisi amiin ki tarah

unhien ke saaye mein phir aaj do dharakate dil
khaamosh honton se kuchh kehne sunne aaye hain
n jaane kitni kashakash se kitni kaavish se
y sote jaagte lamhe chura ke laye hain

yahi faza thi yahi rut yahi zamaana tha
yahin se ham ne mohabbat ki ibtda ki thi
dhadakte dil se larzti hui nigaahon se
hazuure ghaib mein nanhi si iltja ki thi
ke arzu ke kanval khil ke phuul ho jayein
dil o nazar ki duuayein qabuul ho jayein

tassuvaraat ki parchhaaiyaan ubharti hain
tum aa rahi ho zamaane ki aankh se bach kar
nazar jhukaaye hue aur badan churaaye hue
khud apne qadmon ki aahat se jhonpti darti
khud apne saaye ki junmbush se khauf khaye hue
tassuvaraat ki parchhaaiyaan ubharti hain

ravaan hai chhoti si kashti havaaon ke rukh par
nadi ke saaz p mallaah giit gaata hai
tumhaara jism har ik lahar ke jhakole se
meri khuli hui baahon mein jhuul jaata hai
tassuvaraat ki parchhaaiyaan ubharti hain

main phuul taank raha huun tumhaare juude mein
tumhaari aankh massarat se jhukti jaati hai
n jane aaj main kya baat kahne vaala huun
zabaan khushk hai aavaaz rukti jaati hai
tassuvaraat ki parchhaaiyaan ubharti hain

mere gale mein tumhaari gudaaz baahein hain
tumhaare honton p mere labon ke saaye hain
mujhe yaqiin k ham ab kabhi n bichhrein ge
tumhein gumaan hai k ham mil ke bhi paraaye hain
tassuvaraat ki parchhaaiyaan ubharti hain

Sahir

mere palang p bikhri hui kitaabon ko
adaaye a'jzo karam se utha rahi ho tum
suhaag raat jo dholak p gaaye jaate hain
dabe suron mein vohi giit ga rahi ho tum
tassuvaraat ki parchhaaiyaan ubharti hain

voh lamhe kitne dilkash the voh ghariaan kitni pyari thein
voh sehre kitne naazuk the voh lariaan kitni pyaari thein
basti ki har ik shaadaab gali khawaabon ka jaziira thi goya
har mauj-e nafas har mauj-e saba naghmon ka zakhiira thi goya

n gaaha lehkte kheton se taapon ki sadaayein aane lagien
baruud ki bojhal bu le kar pachham se havaayein aane lagien
taa'miir ke raushan chehre par takhriib ka baadal phail gaya
har gaanv mein vahshat naach uthi har shehr mein jangal phail gaya
maghrab ke muhazzab mulkon se kuchh khaki vardi posh aaye
idhlaate hue maghruur aaye lehraate hue madhosh aaye
khaamosh zamiin ke siine mein khaimon ki tanabein garne lagien
makhan si mulaayam raahon par buuton ki khraashein parne lagien
faujon ke bhiyaanak band tale charkhon ki sadaayein duub gayein
jiipon ki sulagati dhuul tale phuulon ki qabaayein duub gayein

insaan ki qiimat girne lagi ajnaas ke bhao chadhne lage
chaupaal ki raunak ghatne lagi bharti ke daftar badhne lage
basti ke sajiile javaan ban ban ke sipahi jaane lage
in jaane vale daston mein ghaiirat bhi gai barnai bhi
maaoon ke javaan bete bhi gaye bahnoon ke chahete bhai bhi

basti p udaasi chhane lagi mailon ki bahaarein khatam huien
aamon ki lachakti shaakhoon se jhuulon ki qataarein khatam huien
dhuul urne lagi baazaron mein bhuukh ugne lagi khilyaanon mein
har chiiz duukanon se ur kar ruuposh hui tehkhanon mein
badhaal gharon ki badhaali badhte badhte janjaal bani
mehngaaii badh kar kaal bani saari basti kangaal bani
charvaahiaan rasta bhuul gaaein panhaariaan panghat chhor gaaein
kitni hi kanvaari ablaaein maan-baap ki chaukhat chhor gaaein

aflaas zada dehqaanon ke hal-bel bike khaliaan bike
jiine ki tamanna ke haathon jiine hi ke sab saamaan bike
kuchh bhi n raha jab bikne ko jismon ki tajaarat hone lagi
khalvat mein bhi jo mamn'u thi vo jalvat mein jasaarat hone lagi
tassuvaraat ki parchhaaiyaan ubharti hain

tum aa rahi ho sar-e aam baal bikhraae hue
hazaar gona malaamat ka baar uthae hue
havas-prast nigahoon ki chiira-dasti se
badan ki jhenpti uriyaaniyaan chiipaae hue
tassuvaraat ki parchhaaiyaan ubharti hain

main shehr ja ke har ik dar ko jhaank aaya huun
kisi jagah meri mehnat ka mol mil n saka
sitam garon ke siyaasi qimaarkhanon mein
alam-nasiib farasat ka mol mil n saka
tassuvaraat ki parchhaaiyaan ubharti hain

tumhaare ghar mein qayaamat ka shor barpa hai
mahaaz-e jang se harkaara taar laya hai
k jis ka zikr tumhein zindagi se pyaara tha
voh bhai narg-e dushman mein kaam aaya hai
tassuvaraat ki parchhaaiyaan ubharti hain

har ek gaam p badnaamioon ke jamghat hain
har ek mor p rusvaaion ke mele hain
n dosti n takaluff n dilbari n khaluus
kisi ka koi nahien aaj sab akele hain
tassuvaraat ki parchhaaiyaan ubharti hain

voh rahguzar jo mere dil ki tarah suuni hai
n jaane tum ko kahan le ke jaane vaali hai
tumhein khariid rahe hain zamiir ke qaatil
ufaq p khuune-tamaanaaye-dil ki laali hai
tassuvaraat ki parchhaaiyaan ubharti hain

Sahir

suraj ke lahu mein lipti hui voh shaam hai ab tak yaad mujhe
chaahat ke sunehre khwaabon ka anjaam hai ab tak yaad mujhe
us shaam mujhe maa'luum hua kheton ki tarah is duniya mein
sehmi hui doshiizaaon ki muskaan bhi bechi jaati hai
us shaam mujhe maa'luum hua is kaargahe zardaari mein
do bholi bhaali ruuhon ki pehchaan bhi bechi jaati hai

us shaam mujhe maa'luum hua jab baap ki kheti chhin jaaye
mamta ke sunehre khwabon ki anmol nishaani bikti hai
us shaam mujhe maa'luum hua jab bhai jang mein kaam aaye
sarmaaye ke qahvakhane mein bahnon ki javaani bikti hai
suraj ke lahu mein lithri hui voh shaam hai ab tak yaad mujhe
chaahat ke sunehre khwabon ka anjaam hai ab tak yaad mujhe

tum aaj hazaron miil yahaan se duur kahiin tanhai mein
ya bazm-e tarab aaraai mein
mere sapne bunti ho gi bethi aaghosh paraii mein

aur main siine mein gham le kar din raat mushaqqat karta huun
jiine ki khatir marta huun
apne fun ko rusva kar ke aghiaar ka daaman bharta huun

majbuur huun main majbuur ho tum majbuur y duniya saari hai
tan ka dukh man par bhaari hai
is daur mein jiine ki qiimat ya daar o rasan ya khvaari hai

main daar o rasan tak ja n saka tum jahd ki hadd tak aa n sakien
chaaha to magar apna n sakien
ham tum do aaisi ruuhein hain jo manzil-e taskiin pa n sakien

jiine ko jiye jaate hain magar saanson mein chitaaein jalti hain
khaamosh vafaein jalti hain
sangiin hakayak zaari mein khwabon ki ridaein jalti hain

aur aaj in peron ke niiche phir do saaye lehraaye hain
phir do dil milne aaye hain
phir maut ki aandhi utthi hai phir jang ke badal chhaaye hain

main soch raha huun in ka bhi apni hi tarah anjaam n ho
in ka bhi junon badnaam n ho
inke bhi muqaddar mein likhi ik khuun mein lithri shaam n ho
suraj ke lahu mein lithri hui voh shaam hai ab tak yaad mujhe
chaahat ke sunehre khwabon ka anjaam hai ab tak yaad mujhe

hamaara pyaar havaadis ki taab la n saka
magar inhein to muraadon ki raat mil jaaye
hamein to kashmakash-e marg-e beimaan hi mili
inhein to jhuumti gaati hayaat mil jaaye

bahut dinon se hai y mashghala siyaasat ka
ke jab javaan hon bachche to qatal ho jaaein
bahut dinon se hai khabat hukam raanon ka
ke duur duur ke mulkon mein qahat bo jaayein

bahut dinon se javaani ke khwaab viiraan hain
bahut dinon se mohabbat panaah dhundhati hai
bahut dinon mein sitam diid shaahraaon mein
nigaar-e ziist ki ismat panaah dhundhuti hai

chalo k aaj sabhi payamaal ruuhon se
kahein k apne har ik zakham ko zubaan kar lein
hamaara raaz hamaara nahien sabhi ka hai
chalo ke saare zamaane ko raazdaan kar lein

chalo ke chal ke siyaasi mukamaron se kahein
ke ham ko jang o jadal ke chalan se nafrat hai
jise lahu ke siva koi rang n raas aaye
hamein hayaat ke us perhan se nafrat hai

kaho k ab koi qaatal agar idhar aaya
to har qadam p zamiin tang hoti jayegi
har ek mauj-e hava rukh badal ke jhapte gi
har ek shaakh rag-e sang hoti jaye gi

utho k aaj har ik jangju se y kah dein
k ham ko kaam ki khatir kalon ki hajat hai
hamein kisi ki zamiin chhiin-ne ka shauq nahien
hamein to apni zamiin par halon ki hajat hai

kaho k ab koi taajar idhar ka rukh n kare
ab is ja koi kanvaari n bechi jayegi
y khet jaag pare uth khari hui faslein
ab is jagah koi kayaari n bechi jayegi

y sarzamiin hai Gautam ki aur Nanak ki
is arz-e paak p vahshi n chal sakein ge kabhi
hamara khuun amanat hai nasl-e nau ke liye
hamaare khuun p lashkar n pal sakein ge kabhi

kaho ke aaj bhi ham agar khmosh rahe
to is damakte hue khaakdaan ki khair nahien
junuun ki dhaali hui atomii balaaon se
zamiin ki khair nahien aasmaan ki khair nahien

guzashta jang mein ghar hi jale magar is baar
a'jab nahien k y tanhaaiyaan bhi jal jayein
guzashta jang mein paikar jale magar is baar
a'jab nahien k y parchhaaiyaan bhi jal jayein
tassuvaraat ki parchhaaiyaan ubharti hain

3
Ghazals
Melody and Meaning

I am the Socrates of the new age
and I don't want to die with parched lips.
Whether it is poison or some flaming wine,
I want the drink of my martyrdom
to be witnessed.

—'Will Stop Relating'

After spending about two years in Delhi as an editor of the literary magazine *Shaahraah*, Sahir arrived in Bombay in early 1950. This was actually Sahir's second visit. The first visit in 1946 was unsuccessful due to a number of reasons, including the impending disorder and disarray because of the Partition. After an initial few years of struggle, he established himself as a leading film lyricist.

Sahir always believed that his entry into films made him a better poet because it pushed him towards higher thresholds of personal creativity. This was not an easy transition. The hands of a film lyricist are tied by the requirements of the story as well as the demands of the music director, who sets the lyrics to music, which are sung to the accompaniment of an orchestra. But Sahir overcame these constraints in more than one way. First, he decided to bring into the film world the literary jewels of his highly acclaimed literary work, *Talkhiyaan*. Second, even when he wrote a new piece for a film, he did not compromise its literary quality. Ibrahim Jalees, a film writer, reinforces this view:

Traditionally, in the film industry music directors had a much higher profile than a song writer. Film distributors would inquire before buying a film for release, 'Who is the music director? Naushad, S.D. Burman, Shankar-Jaikishan? Who?' No distributor ever asked the name of a song writer. But Sahir and Majrooh [Sultanpuri] changed this. When they wrote the songs, no one asked about the music director.[1]

Jan Nisar Akhtar, who himself wrote for films, summed up Sahir's contribution to upgrading the quality of film lyrics in the following words:

There is no doubt that Sahir performed a miracle by giving to film songs ... a social and political awakening. It was a different kind of a task and it required a lot of courage. Unlike many other lyricists, he did not drown himself in the lower depths of traditional film songs. He brought forth beauty, sensibility, and the feelings associated with the joys of lovers' union and the pangs of separation. He did not degrade himself, nor did he betray the progressive movement, which he thought was represented in his work, or the people who expected from him a literary flavour in whatever he penned. This was the work of a poet who was aware of his responsibility and, on this achievement, I offer him my heartiest congratulations.[2]

Sahir was a poet of the nazm form. He attained excellence in this genre at an early age. Reading his early poems, one gets the feeling that the nazm came to him naturally. The flow of words was like water gushing from a fountain, and thoughts were clearly expressed using innovative similes and metaphors. In terms of the lyrical quality, every poem that he wrote contained some flavour of ghazal, as he often used *qaafiya* (the rhyming syllable at the end of a two-line verse) and *radiif* (words that are repeated after rhyme), the two most essential elements of a ghazal. Here is an example:

ik dil tha jo pahle hi tujhe saunp diya tha
y jaan bhi ai jaan-e ada saath liye ja

In this couplet, *ada* is qaafiya and *saath liye ja* is radiif.

[1] Ibrahim Jalees, '*Abdul Hayee Se Sahir Ludhianvi*', *Adab Saaz*, 12–14, 2010: 61.

[2] Jan Nisar Akhtar, '*Giiton Ka Rasiya*', *Fan aur Shakhsiyat*, 17–18, 1985: 393–8.

When Sahir transitioned to film song writing, the task was thus less challenging for him.

There is a view among people that nazm poets do not generally become good ghazal poets. The poet who writes a poem works on a very wide canvas while enjoying a lot of freedom. A poem can be written in free verse, blank verse, or by selecting any of the metrical patterns. The famous English poet and critic Alexander Pope wrote in *An Essay on Criticism*:

True ease in writing comes from art, not chance,
As those move easiest who have learned to dance.[3]

Dancing has rules, but good dancers improvise a lot. This is the artistic freedom that a nazm poet enjoys, and Sahir provides ample evidence of this.

Ghazal writing, on the other hand, is restrictive. Whatever the poet has to say, he has to say in two short lines, which should be well rhymed and contain a thought that is significant in itself. Ghazal writing is an art that requires disciplined training and practice. Literary critic Majnun Gorakhpuri presented a balanced assessment of Sahir's nazm and ghazal poetry when he wrote:

Poetry came naturally to Sahir, and it came with a force, so that whether he was writing a nazm or a ghazal he accomplished the task with great artistic flair. He knew how to present a confluence of inner feelings and outer influences and this fusion is seen in everything he wrote. Whether it was a nazm or a ghazal, Sahir never let go the special quality known as *ghazliat* [the quality of lyricism traditionally associated with composing an ode] or *taghazzul* [the art of versification].[4]

In this chapter, we present a wide selection of Sahir's ghazals. Several of them were written for films. Most of them were set to music

[3] Mary Oliver, *Rules for the Dance* (New York: Houghton Mifflin Company, 1998), 81.

[4] Majnun Gorakhpuri, '*Jadeed Ghazal Pakistan aur Hindustan Mein*', *Fanuun*, Ghazal Number, 1969: 15.

by highly talented music directors like S.D. Burman, and sung by exceptional singers like Mohammad Rafi, Talat Mahmood, Lata Mangeshkar, and Asha Bhosle.

A special attribute of Sahir's ghazal writing that needs to be highlighted is that a majority of his ghazals have a single theme, or they present a particular scene, an idea, an incident, a situation. Therefore, there is a flow of thought that is consistent from the first couplet to the last. This is not the norm for ghazal writing; among the great poets only Hasrat Mohani and Momin have used this approach successfully. Sahir finds comfort in this because he is primarily a poet of the nazm, and also writing for films might have required this.

The reader may also notice that in this chapter we deviate from our approach of providing English translations before the Urdu text, as seen in Chapters 1 and 2. Unlike a poem—which encapsulates a single idea, perspective, or an experience comparable to the creation of a painting or a piece of sculpture—a ghazal consists of couplets that are like mini poems and have the capacity to stand alone as a literary creation. The Urdu text followed by the English translation for each couplet, it is felt, will enhance the reading experience.

Those With Loving Hearts

Am I the only one or are there others too? We confront this question while facing different life situations. There is love in my heart. But what about others? I am disenchanted with the world. But what about others? We connect with others in ways that are not easy to perceive. The social norms easily permit sharing of good thoughts and of joys and celebrations while discouraging sharing of one's pain. This is because the unwritten rule says that one's pain is like no one else's. This often creates alienation and ennui. Sahir ends the ghazal with a barb for the chief of the morality establishment, often a target for the progressive poets because of his duplicitous character. Those who preach morality often fail the test of fidelity to their principles. This is an example of a complicating situation: people do not reveal their true selves and their true preferences.

Ahl-e Dil

ahl-e dil aur bhi hain ahl-e vafa aur bhi hain
ek ham hi nahien duniya se khafa aur bhi hain

There are those with loving hearts
and those who value
being true to their love.
I'm not the only one
disenchanted with the world,
there are others too.

ham p hi khatam nahien maslak-e shoriida-sari
chaak dil aur bhi hain chaak qaba aur bhi hain

I'm not the only one
who can claim madness of love,
there are others too
with broken hearts and torn garments.

kya hua gar mere yaaron ki zabaanein chup hain
mere shaahid mere yaaron ke siva aur bhi hain

Never mind,
my friends have their tongues tied.
My witnesses include people
other than my own friends.

sar salaamat hai to kya sang-e malaamat ki kami
jaan baaqi hai to paikaan-e qaza aur bhi hain

Even if the head is in the right place,
there will be no shortage
of censure.
If you are still alive
you won't feel a dearth of fatal arrows.

munsif-e shahr ki vahdat p n harf aa jaaye
log kahte hain k arbaab-e jafa aur bhi hain

I don't want the blame to fall
on the chief of the city's morality police,
I have heard there are many others
who fail the test of fidelity as well.

Splendid

This ghazal, which was sung by Mohammad Rafi for the 1965 film *Kaajal*, hits you like a gust of morning breeze with its freshness. There is nothing which is complicated. If a good thing happens, it leads to good outcomes. But still there are always concerns that are not within one's immediate control. How do others judge our actions? The very thought imposes a burden. We need to go beyond the ideas of right and wrong and try to unburden ourselves. The last couplet touches on a theme common in Urdu love poetry. Love always leads to ruination in which the beloved plays a part. The poet concedes the point but with a twist suggests that blame should fall on something else. When we finish reading this ghazal, this one thought lingers in our minds: splendid!

Achha

y zulf agar khul ke bikhar jaaye to achcha
is raat ki taqdiir sanvar jaaye to achcha

Splendid—
if your curly locks
come undone.
Splendid—
if the fate of this night
is embellished.

jis tarah se thori si tere saath kati hai
baaqi bhi isi tarah guzar jaaye to achcha

188

Splendid—
if I could spend
the rest of the night
in the same way that I have passed
a small part of it with you.

duniya ki nigaahon mein bhala kya hai bura kya
y bojh agar dil se utar jaaye to achcha

Splendid—
if I can lift the burden
of right and wrong
that the world
has imposed on me.

vaise to tumhiin ne mujhe barbaad kiya hai
ilzaam kisi aur ke sar jaaye to achcha

Splendid—
if I can blame someone else
for my ruination,
though this work has been accomplished
by you alone.

These Valleys

This ghazal, written for the 1963 movie *Aaj Aur Kal* and sung by Mohammad Rafi, is the perfect example of the complete amalgamation of nature and romance. Standing in the midst of beautiful valleys, the poet is sending a message to his beloved: 'Come, I'm missing you. Not only me, but everything around me wants you. The flowers are waiting for an opportunity to kiss your lips. The black rain clouds are begging to taste the fragrance of your black tresses. The flowing stream is yearning to wet your purplish feet. It is not only nature, but the prayers of every loving heart want you.' Only Sahir could write a ghazal like this!

Y Vaadiyaan

y vaadiyaan y fazaaein bula rahi hain tumhein
khamoshiyon ki sadaaein bula rahi hain tumhein

These valleys and these environs
are calling you.
Voices tucked away in these silences
are calling you.

taras rahe hain javaan phuul hont chhune ko
machal machal ke havaaein bula rahi hain tumhein

Pitiable is the condition
of buds while yearning
to touch your lips.
Restless currents of air
are calling you.

tumhaari zulfon se khushbu ki bhiik lene do
jhuki jhuki si ghataein bula rahi hain tumhein

To gain the offering
of the fragrance of your tresses,
bowed rain clouds
are calling you.

hasiin champaii pairon ko jab se dekha hai
nadi ki mast adaayein bula rahi hain tumhein

After they saw your purplish feet,
lovely as they are,
the drunken ways of the flowing stream
are calling you.

mera kaha n suno un ki baat to sun lo
har ek dil ki duaayein bula rahi hain tumhein

Don't pay attention to what I say,
but you must listen
to the prayers of each and every heart
calling you.

I'll Sever All Ties

This is a non-thematic ghazal in the sense that each couplet presents an idea that is unique and different. But the common thread through them all is the feel of history and mythology, together with the poet's personal resolve to face all kinds of situations with a strong determination. *Qayaamat* (apocalypse), which is a religious concept, is a frightening possibility for some but not for the poet, who is ready to confront even the worst scenarios. He considers himself the Socrates of the new age who wants to make his martyrdom apparent. This is important in a world where people are not playing their assigned roles. Friends are no longer good friends, enemies are no longer good enemies. Preachers try to reform others while they themselves live in their own 'alley of degradation'. The ghazal ends with a call to revolution, a revolt against ignorance sustained by ruling monarchs who collude with the religious establishment to keep things under control.

Tor Lein Ge

tor lein ge har ik shai se rishta tor dene ki naubat to aaye
ham qayaamat ke khud muntazir hain par kisi din qayaamat to aaye

I will sever my ties with everything
if it comes to that.
I am awaiting the apocalypse,
let my expectations be fulfilled.

ham bhi suqraat hain a'hd-e nau ke tashna lab hi n mar jaayein yaaro
zahr ho ya mai-e aatiishein ho koi jaam-e shahadat to aaye

I am the Socrates of the new age
and I don't want to die with parched lips.

Whether it is poison or some flaming wine,
I want the drink of my martyrdom
to be witnessed.

ek tahziib hai dosti ki ek mai'yaar hai dushmani ka
doston ne muravvat n siikhi dushmanon ko adaavat to aaye

There is an etiquette to friendship
and a measure of enmity.
Friends didn't learn to be kind.
At least enemies should learn
to be better foes.

ilm o tahziib taariikh o mantiq log sochein ge in mas'alon par
zindagi ke mashaqqat kade mein koi a'hd-e faraaghat to aaye

People who know history and logic
would reflect on these matters
but let there be some freedom
from worries in this life of constant hardship
and suffering.

rind raaste mein aankhein bichhaaein jo kahe bin sune maan jaayein
naaseh-e nek tiinat kisi shab suu-e kuu-e malaamat to aaye

The dissolute would blindly believe
what they are told,
but I want preachers with good intent
to visit the lane where humiliation occurs.

kaanp utthein qasr-e shaahi ke gumbad thartharaaye zamiin ma'badon ki
kuucha gardon ki vahshat to jaage gham zadon ko baghavat to aaye

Let the domes of royal palaces tremble
and the earth under temples
quake.

Let those who aimlessly wander
show their rising wildness
and learn how to revolt.

It is Better to Die

This ghazal, written for the 1955 film *House No. 44*, was sung by
Hemant Kumar. It is a verse of total resignation, of giving up on life.
For the poet, all kinds of pain are bearable, but not the pain of life
without love. If you love tragedy, you will cherish this ghazal.

Behtar Hai K Mar Jaayein

teri duniya mein jiine se to behtar hai k mar jaayein
vohi aansu vohi aahein vohi gham hai jidhar jaaein

It is better to die than to live
in this world of yours.
Wherever I go,
it is the same tears, the same sighs,
and the same sadness.

koi to aisa ghar hota jahaan se pyaar mil jaata
vohi begaane chehre hain jahaan jaaein jidhar jaayein

I wish there were
at least one hearth
where I could find love!
Wherever I go,
I see unfamiliar faces.

are o aasmaan vaale bata is mein bura kya hai
khushi ke chaar jhonke gar idhar se bhi guzar jaayein

O resident of the sky,
tell me, would it be wrong
if four drifts of happiness

passed by the place
where I stand?

Tired

This ghazal was first recited by Mohammad Rafi without any music in his powerful melodious voice for the 1957 movie *Pyaasa*, and then by Asha Bhosle a year later for the film *Lighthouse*. Saying no to life requires courage. What if nothing is working? What if you have reached a dead end? What if your love story has ended in a way that you can't even talk about it? Although the situation is bad, not all hope is lost. The depressed heart can rise again. But it is not certain. The battle one fights on a daily basis might go on, or it might just end.

Tang Aa Chuke Hain

tang aa chuke hain kashmakash-e zindagi se ham
thukra n dein jahaan ko kahiin be dili se ham

I am tired of the struggles
of my day-to-day life.
I have reached a point
where I'm ready
to uncaringly say no
to everything
this world has to offer.

maayuusi-e ma'aal-e mohabbat n puuchhiye
apnon se pesh aaye hain begaanagi se ham

Don't ask me
about the sad end
of my love story.
I'm coming across
as unfeeling to those
who are dear to me.

lo aaj ham ne tor diya rishta-e ummiid
lo ab kabhi gila n karein ge kisi se ham

Today I broke
my connection
with the bond of hope.
Now I shall not complain
about anything.

ubhrein ge ek baar abhi dil ke valvale
go dab gaye hain baar-e gham-e zindagi se ham

My depressed heart
shall rise once again,
though I feel warped
by the burden
of the sorrows of life.

gar zindagi mein mil gaye phir ittifaaq se
puuchhen ge apna haal teri bebasi se ham

If we met again by chance in life,
I shall enquire about my own well-being
through the lens of your helplessness.

allah re freb-e mashiyyat k aaj tak
duniya ke zulm sahte rahe khaamushi se ham

Only god can reveal
the secret of how
I was able to suffer
the cruelties of the world
in such great silence.

Let Us Talk

The thread that binds this ghazal is the radiif *'baat karein'*—'let us
talk'. We know that speech is made up of words and words have

meanings that clarify. This is a traditional view. Not everyone agrees with this. Bedil, the Indian poet who wrote in Persian, once said that a good couplet has no meaning. What he meant was that goodness in this case rests with not having any fixed meaning. Goodness also makes it something alive or living so that meaning will change over time. The same is true of what we speak. What is punishment? What is reward? How do we express desire? How do we talk about god or gods? How do we talk about beauty? The words we choose to convey something may not mean the same to the listener. Or these meanings might change over time. But there is no alternative to speech or talk. It should never stop. When it stops, the world comes to a standstill.

Baat Karein

saza ka haal sunaayein jaza ki baat karein
khuda mila ho jinhein vo khuda ki baat karein

Let us talk about the context
of our retributions and rewards.
Those who found god
should talk about their god.

unhein pata bhi chale aur vo khafa bhi n hon
is ehtiyaat se kya muddaa'a k baat karein

She gets to know it
but shows no annoyance.
Let us talk about our desire
with great caution.

hamaare a'hd ki tahziib mein qaba hi nahien
agar qaba ho to band-e qaba ki baat karein

In the civilized tenor of our age
it is hard to find an apparel.

If we find one, then let us talk
about the apparel's knot.[5]

har ek daur ka mazhab naya khuda laaya
karein to ham bhi magar kis khuda ki baat karein

Each period of human history
gave us a new vision of god.
Let us talk about god—
but which god should we talk about?

vafa shi'aar kayi hain koi hasiin bhi to ho
chalo phir aaj usi bevafa ki baat karein

There are many
who proclaim their sincerity,
but are they beautiful?
Today, let us talk once again
about the graceful one
who lacked constancy.

All Things

This ghazal, written for the 1971 movie *Sansaar* and sung by Mahindra
Kapoor, is a meditation on the world in which we live. The world is
maya, says Vedanta. Everything in this world is without any essence,
says Nagarjuna, the great Buddhist philosopher. We come from fog,
the poet says, and then disappear into another cloud of fog. No one
has succeeded in resolving this mystery.

Sansar Ki Har Shai

sansaar ki har shai ka itna hi fasana hai
ik dhundh se aana hai ik dhundh mein jana hai

---

[5] Here 'apparel' refers to one's standing in society; 'knot' to the pre-British era
when there were no buttons. To remove an apparel, one had to loosen all the knots.

Everything around us
has a story to tell.
We come from a cloud of fog
and then disappear
into another cloud of fog.

y raah kahaan se hai y raah kahaan tak hai
y raaz koi raahi samjha hai n jaana hai

From where does
this path come
and where does it go?
No traveller on this path
has resolved this mystery.

ik pal ki palak par hai thahri hui y duniya
ik palak jhapapne tak har khel suhaana hai

This world rests
on the eyelid of a moment.
Until that eye blinks,
this play looks fine.

kya jaane koi kis par kis mo-r par kya biite
is raah mein ai raahi har mo-r bahana hai

No one knows
what would happen
to any one of us
at any moment.
On this path
every bend in the way
is a kind of an excuse.

ham log khilauna hain ik aise khilari ka
jis ko abhi sadiyon tak y khel rachaana hai

We are playthings of a player
who is happy to play
this game for centuries to come.

The Seat of the Soul

Knowledge is important for a productive life. But what is knowledge made of? It is made up of facts, assumptions, ideas, concepts, theories, and constructs. What about the unknown, which is not apparent, and is beneath the layers of our consciousness? Philosophers and psychologists have tried to grapple with this issue over time. Plato talked about the shadows we see from inside the cave, meaning that our knowledge about the real world is imperfect. Swiss psychologist Carl Jung wrote about the role that the unconscious plays in charting our lives, about the collective unconscious showing the influence of myths and archetypes on human behaviour. This is the point that Sahir is trying to get across. Life for a person who has seen one defeat after another is a cup of poison, but that is not the essence of life. Life is not just a sum total of our sorrows. It is more than that. Life's potential is limitless. One needs the courage and emotional stability to discover this.

Nafas Ki Loch Mein

nafas ke loch mein ram hi nahien kuchh aur bhi hai
hayaat saaghar-e sam hi nahien kuchh aur bhi hai

In the seat of the soul
there is something more
than its resilience.
Life is not just
a cup of poison.
It is something more.

teri nigaah mere gham ki paasdaar sahi
meri nigaah mein gham hi nahien kuchh aur bhi hai

Your gaze shows
respect for my sorrow.
But in my eyes,
it is not just sorrow.
It is something more.

mere nadiim mohabbat ki rif'aton se n gir
buland baam-e haram hi nahien kuchh aur bhi hai

Don't fall down
from the heights of love,
dear friend.
It is not just Kaba's roof.[6]
It is something more.

y ijtinaab hai aks-e shuu'ur-e mahbuubi
y ihtiyaat-e sitam hi nahien kuchh aur bhi hai

I refrain from saying anything
about the reflection
of the consciousness of my beloved.
It is not just an awareness of tyranny.
It is something more.

idhar bhi ek uchat-ti nazar ki duniya mein
farogh-e mahfil-e jam hi nahien kuchh aur bhi hai

With my quick glance at the world
I see not only assemblies
of Jamshed's followers,[7]
drinking and enjoying.
There is something more.

---

[6] Kaba is the place where Muslims go for pilgrimage. Its dome is of great height. But love is higher than Kaba's dome.

[7] Jamshed was a Persian mythological figure who could see the whole universe in his cup of wine.

naye jahaan basaaye hain fikr-e aadam ne
ab is zamiin p iram hi nahien kuchh aur bhi hai

Human imagination
has populated new worlds.
Now on this earth of ours
there are not only glimpses
of cities of paradise,
there is something more.

mere shuu'ur ko aavaara kar diya jis ne
voh marg-e shaadi o gham hi nahien kuchh aur bhi hai

That which has
liberated my consciousness
is not just the death of happiness
and sorrow.
It is something more.

Gave Up Loving

Our life goes through different transitions. We fall in love, or love takes us prisoner. But when it does not work, when everything hits a wall, when love meets with indifference, there is a time for change. In Urdu poetry this is not the norm. Love is an all-consuming fire. To fall in love is to willingly choose a very painful death. But Sahir, being a progressive poet, deviates from the poetic tradition. Breaking up is fine, he says, the lover can take this poison pill and still survive.

This beautiful ghazal was sung by Talat Mahmood in his mellifluous voice for the 1952 movie *Doraha*. This was a very difficult time for Sahir, when he was struggling to get a break in the film industry. At novelist Krishan Chander's request, Prem Dhawan, who was himself a lyricist and production manager for the film, agreed to recommend this ghazal, which had been published in *Talkhiyaan*, to Anil Biswas, who was the film's music director. Talat's rendition of Sahir's words made this an evergreen ghazal of Hindi cinema.

Mohabbat Tark Ki Main Ne

mohabbat tark ki main ne garebaan si liya main ne
zamaane ab to khush ho zahr y bhi pi liya main ne

I gave up loving you
and I stitched my collar.[8]
People of the world,
are you happy now?
I did take this poison.

abhi zinda huun lekin sochta rahta huun khalvat mein
k ab tak kis tamanna ke sahaare ji liya main ne

I am still alive
but I ponder in my solitude,
What were those desires
that helped me
keep on living?

unhein apna nahien sakta magar itna bhi kya kam hai
k kuchh muddat hasiin khwaabon mein kho kar ji liya main ne

I can't embrace them,
but it is not easy
living in my alluring dreams
for some time
to escape
life's harsher realities.

bas ab to daaman-e dil chhor do bekaar ummido
bahut dukh sah liye main ne bahut din ji liya main ne

O useless hopes,
now you should leave the hem

---

[8] Tearing your collar is a mark of insanity; stitching it up refers to regaining it.

of my heart alone.
I have suffered enough pain.
I have lived for many days.

Love ... Sometimes

This ghazal is a marvel of poetic lyricism, with each couplet flawlessly flowing into the next. The content itself is nothing unique. It is an idea that other poets have also explored, but Sahir brings some newness by constructing this ghazal in a way that the first line talks about common life events: love comes to us sparingly, people show indifference at times, flowers bloom every day, you can't live in loneliness for ever, we lose friends in the tumult of life, etc. The second line reinforces the argument with more specificity. Just read this ghazal for the magic of its lyrical quality. You can also listen to the soundtrack of the 1968 movie *Aankhein* for this melody, which was sung by Lata Mangeshkar.

Mohabbat Kabhi Kabhi

milti hai zindagi mein mohabbat kabhi kabhi
hoti hai dilbaron ki a'naayat kabhi kabhi

Love comes
in life, but not so often.
Sweethearts show their kindness,
but not so often.

sharma ke munh n pher nazar ke savaal par
laati hai aise mo-r p qismat kabhi kabhi

Don't feel shy
and turn your face around
when I want to look at you.
Our fate brings us
to such interchanges,
but not so often.

khulte nahien hain roz dariiche bahaar ke
aati hai jaan-e man y qayaamat kabhi kabhi

The vistas of spring
do not open up every day.
This apocalypse happens,
my love, but not so often.

tanha n kat sakein ge javaani ke raaste
pesh aaegi kisi ki zaruurat kabhi kabhi

The paths of youth
call for company.
We shall need this,
but not so often.

phir kho n jaaein ham kahiin duniya ki bhiid mein
milti hai paas aane ki mohlat kabhi kabhi

We don't wish to get lost
once again
in this worldly crowd.
We get the chance
to get close to someone,
but not so often.

I am Alive

This ghazal is not about tender relationships such as the lover's complaints about the beloved and her indifference. It is written by Sahir the revolutionary. The law is the tyrant's weapon, and so it always favours the establishment. In this situation, it is important for the revolutionary to announce his 'aliveness'—his availability for torture and hanging. In the end, the revolutionary wins by dying and the tyrannical regime loses by its use of force.

Main Zinda Huun

main zinda huun y mushtahar kiijiye
mere qaatilon ko khabar kiijiye

I am alive.
Let this be proclaimed.
Let my murderers know this.

zamiin sakht hai aasmaan duur hai
basar ho sake to basar kiijiye

The ground is hard
and the sky is far away.
If we can,
let us try to live like this.

vohi zulm baar-e digar hai to phir
vohi jurm baar-e digar kiijiye

If others are oppressed.
Let us commit the same crime,
by oppressing those
who oppress.

sitam ke bahut se hain radd-e amal
zaruuri nahien chashm tar kiijiye

There are many ways
to respond to tyranny.
It is not necessary
to wet our eyes.

qafas torna baa'd ki baat hai
abhi khwaahish-e baal o par kiijiye

There will be time
to break the prison.

For the time being,
let us pray
for feathers and wings.

Lips are Sealed

This ghazal takes off from the ideas in the last ghazal. The difference is the context, which is independent India in this case. The poet sees some improvements since the British yoke was shed. But he feels that the country's leaders are not acting the way they should. Their exhibitionist display of patriotism has made the very act dishonourable, not because they are losing power and influence but because they are promoting disunity and disharmony. Although there are all kinds of constraints on 'speaking truth to power', those who love their country should speak up without any fear.

Lab Par Paabandi

lab p paabandi to hai ehsaas par pehra to hai
phir bhi ahl-e dil ko ahvaal-e bashar kahna to hai

Our lips are sealed
and feelings are under watch
but those who have a heart
have to chronicle
the human condition.

khuun-e a'daa se n ho khuun-e shahidaan hi se ho
kuchh n kuchh is daur mein rang-e chaman nikhra to hai

If not with the blood of enemies,
at least with the blood of martyrs.
We see some difference
in the way the garden blossoms
these days.

apni ghairat bech daalein apna maslak chhor dein
rahnumaaon mein bhi kuchh logon ka y mansha to hai

Let them sell their honour
and let them change
the rules of their conduct.
Among leaders too
there is such an intent taking shape.

hai jinhein sab se ziyaada daa'va-e hubb-e vatan
aaj un ki vajh se hubb-e vatan rusva to hai

Those who loudly proclaim
their love of the country
have made love of the land
look like a dishonourable act.

bujh rahe hain ek ik kar ke aqiidon ke diye
is andhere ka bhi lekin saamna karna to hai

The lights of belief systems
are slowly getting doused.
Like it or not,
we have to confront
this coming darkness.

jhuut kyun bolein farogh-e maslahat ke naam par
zindagi pyaari sahi lekin hamein marna to hai

Why should we tell a lie
to promote a compromise?
Life is dear to us,
but we must die one day.

Couldn't Do It

In this ghazal the poet returns to self-examination, and what he finds
is extremely discouraging: life is a series of regrets and failures. For

once the heart loses its verve, it is very hard to regain the rhythm. Once you are on a road that goes downhill, it requires great effort to break loose of the inertia that sets in and reverse the direction of your movement.

N Kar Sake

khud-daariyon ke khuun ko arzaan n kar sake
ham apne jauharon ko numaayaan n kar sake

My passion for my self-esteem
didn't allow me
to do certain things,
though it meant
that my jewel-like talents
stayed unexpressed.

ho kar khraab-e mai tere gham to bhula diye
lekin gham-e hayaat ka darmaan n kar sake

By choosing wine
I overcame the grief
of losing you,
but that didn't help me
defeat the grief of life itself.

tuuta tilism-e a'hd-e mohabbat kuchh is tarah
phir aarzu ki sham'a firozaan n kar sake

The spell
of my declaration of love
broke in such a way
that I could never light
the candle of longing again.

har shai qariib aa ke kashish apni kho gayi
voh bhi ilaaj-e shauq-e gurezaan n kar sake

All things
on a closer look
lost their appeal—
and even that was not enough
to regain that which was lost.

kis darja dilshikan the mohabbat ke haadse
ham zindagi mein phir koi armaan n kar sake

So disheartening
were the circumstances
of our love affair
that I spent my whole life
without showing
any longing again.

maayuusiyon ne chhiin liye dil ke valvale
vo bhi nashaat-e ruuh ka saamaan n kar sake

Facing
one disappointment after another
killed my heart's passion,
but even that did not
help my soul
gain its rhythm again.

The Crime of Love

This ghazal, written for the 1963 film *Taj Mahal* and sung by Lata Mangeshkar, is a great pleasure to read. The thought pattern is traditional, and typical of Urdu poetry: lovers unabashedly declaring their love for each other in the face of all kinds of censure. The lover's declaration at the end says it all: 'We have given our heart/and signed the pledge of love./Now you can fondly give us the punishment/you think we deserve.'

Jurm-e Ulfat

jurm-e ulfat p hamein log saza dete hain
kaise nadaan hain sho'alon ko hava dete hain

People punish us
for the crime of love.
How innocent are those
who fan the flames?

ham se divaane kahin tark-e vafa karte hain
jaan jaaye k rahe baat nibha lete hain

Crazy lovers like us
would never stop loving.
We can sacrifice our breath
but we shall never break promises.

aap daulat ke taraazu mein dilon ko tolein
ham mohabbat se mohabbat ka sila dete hain

You measure hearts
on the same scale as wealth.
We return the gift of love
with love.

takht kya chiiz hai laal-o javaahar kya hain
i'shq vaale to khudaaii bhi luta dete hain

Thrones, rubies, and jewels
hold no attraction for us.
Those who love
are willing to give up
their divinity.

ham ne dil de bhi diya a'hd-e vafa le bhi liya
aap ab shauq se de lein jo saza dete hain

We have given our heart
and signed the pledge of love.
Now you can fondly give us the punishment
you think we deserve.

The Story of My Love

This ghazal is not completely thematic, and it seems to wander in terms of its focus. The forsaken lover defends his behaviour in the face of his beloved's unfaithfulness. The last four couplets make this ghazal truly remarkable and they are worth reading more than once.

Daastaan-e Shauq

jab kabhi un ki tavajjoh mein kami paayi gayi
az sar-e nau daastaan-e shauq dohraayi gayi

Whenever I found
her interest dwindling,
I had to recite
the story of my love
right from the start.

bik gae jab tere lab phir tujh ko kya shikva agar
zindgaani baada o saaghar se bahlaayi gayi

Having sold your charms,
how can you complain
that I spent my life
in the company
of wine and goblets?

ai gham-e duniya tujhe kya i'lm tere vaaste
kin bahaanon se tabii'at raah par laayi gayi

Sorrows of the world,
you have no idea

of how much work it took
to bring my state of mind
back on track.

ham karein tark-e vafa achha chalo yuun hi sahi
aur agar tark-e vafa se bhi n rusvaayi gayi

Should I stop loving her?
I can do that.
But if that does not lessen my notoriety,
then what would?

kaise kaise chashm o aariz gard-e gham se bujh gaye
kaise kaise paikaron ki shaan-e zebaayi gayi

How many bright eyes
and glowing cheeks
have lost their brilliance
and how many images of beauty
have lost their ornamentations!

dil ki dharkan mein tavazun aa chala hai khair ho
meri nazrein bujh gaiyein ya teri raa'naayi gayi

My heart
is finally throbbing steadily.
Did my eyes
lose their sight
or did you lose
your loveliness?

un ka gham un ka tasavvar un ke shikve ab kahaan
ab to ye baatein bhi ai dil ho gayein aayi gayi

The grief of losing her,
memories left behind,

and complaints.
Even these things, my heart,
are stories
that have come and gone.

jurrat-e insaan p go taadiib ke pehre rahe
fitrat-e insaan ko kab zanjiir pahnaayi gayi

The courage of man
was already constrained
and kept under check.
When was the nature of man
fettered and shackled?

What Should I Do?

This short ghazal of only four couplets, sung by Mohammad Rafi for
the 1963 movie *Aaj Aur Kal*, flawlessly mixes natural beauty with
romance. Notice the two couplets in the middle: 'The moonlit night/
is spreading its perfume/around the arms of the trees./My thoughts
are touching/the peaks of restlessness.' And this melds into the presence
of the one who is desired: 'My breath is blending/with the redolence/of
another breath./Some hands are reaching out/to the edge of my
clothes.'

Kya Karein

itni hasiin itni javaan raat kya karein
jaage hain kuchh a'jiib se jazbaat kya karein

What should I do?
This beautiful
and youthful night
has rekindled
some strange emotions!

peron ke baazuon mein mahakti hai chaandni
bechain ho rahe hain khayaalaat kya karein

The moonlit night
is spreading its perfume
around the arms of the trees.
My thoughts are touching
the peaks of restlessness.

sanson mein ghul rahi hai kisi ki mahak
daaman ko chhu raha hai koi haath kya karein

My breath is blending
with the redolence
of another breath.
Some hands are reaching out
to the edge of my clothes.

shaayad tumhaare aane se y bhed khul sake
hairaan hain k aaj nayi baat kya karein

Maybe this mystery
will be resolved
by your arrival.
I wonder
if I should start
a new conversation.
What should I do?

The Caravans of Spring

This non-thematic ghazal is a priceless specimen of traditional Urdu poetry where each couplet contains a new idea or a situation and the poet weaves the couplet as an artist paints a picture. When spring is over, it leaves behind dried leaves and barren trees—things that can be compared with living organisms suffering wounds. In the second couplet, the comparison of 'heart-stealing faces' with 'flowers of the spring' is quite innovative. The fourth couplet has two very powerful images: 'clothes of the rain clouds' and the 'bodies made of shards of light'. The joy of reading this ghazal stays long after you have read the last couplet.

Qaafle Bahaaron Ke

is taraf se guzre the qaafile bahaaron ke
aaj tak sulagte hain zakhm rahguzaaron ke

The caravans of spring
passed in this direction.
The wounds of the travellers
are smouldering
until this day.

gesuon ki chhaanv mein dilnavaaz chehre hain
ya hasiin dhundhulkon mein phuul hain bahaaron ke

In the shadows of tresses
there are heart-stealing faces.
Or am I seeing in this alluring mist
flowers of the spring?

khalvaton ke shaidaaii khalvaton mein khulte hain
ham se puuchh kar dekho raaz pardah-daaron ke

Those who love solitude,
open up only in solitude.
You should ask me the secrets of those
who live behind veils.

pehle hans ke milte hain phir nazar churaate hain
aashna sifat hain log ajnabi dayaaron ke

First, they meet you smiling
and then they turn their eyes away.

Extremely friendly are the people
of unknown dominions.

tum ne sirf chaaha hai ham ne chhu ke dekhe hain
pairahan ghataaon ke jism barq paaron ke

You only desired it,
but I have touched and seen
the clothes of the rain clouds
and the bodies made of shards of light.

shugl-e mai parasti go jashn-e namuraadi tha
yuun bhi kat gaye kuchh din tere sogvaaron ke

The celebration of wine drinking
was in fact a moment of defeat.
This is how your mourners
passed their time of life.

Not Yet

This ghazal has some amazing couplets, but it is best remembered for
the third one. Poets are the dreamers of a new world where love can
not only survive but flourish. But in real life, love is constrained when
there are social divisions based on caste, religion, income, etc. Love
is restrained when the establishment (religious or political) decides
whom you can love. Poets can dream about an ideal world, but they
can't bring it into being. Only a social revolution can create this new
world.

Nahien

havas nasiib nazar ko kahien qaraar nahien
main muntazir huun magar tera intizaar nahien

Eyes destined to pursue
lustful ways lack stillness.

Though I'm waiting,
I don't expect you
to show up.

hamiin se rang-e gulistaan hamiin se rang-e bahaar
hamiin ko nazm-e gulistaan p ikhtiyaar nahien

I provide colour
for the garden's beauty
and spring's brilliance
but I have no control
over how the garden's verse
is composed.

abhi n chher mohabbat ke giit ai mutrib
abhi hayaat ka maahaul khush gavaar nahien

Minstrel,
please do not start to sing
the songs of love yet.
The circumstances
are not agreeable
for this right now.

tumhaare a'hd-e vafa ko main a'hd kya samjhuun
mujhe khud apni mohabbat p e'tibaar nahien

What can I make
of your declaration
of constancy?
I have no confidence
in my own ability
to love you.

n jaane kitne gile is mein muztarib hain nadiim
voh ek dil jo kisi ka gila guzaar nahien

I wonder how many complaints
are restlessly hiding in this, my friend.
The heart that does not nurse
any complaint against anyone.

gurez ka nahien qaail hayaat se lekin
jo sach kahun k mujhe maut naagavaar nahien

I'm not running away from life
but to tell you the truth:
I don't find death distressing,
dreadful, or invidious.

y kis maqaam p pahuncha diya zamaane ne
k ab hayaat p tera bhi ikhtiyaar nahien

To what point
have my life's circumstances
brought me?
Now even you don't control
how I live the rest of my life.

Doesn't Work the Way I Wish

Each couplet of this traditional ghazal is worth reading and reflecting upon. Things don't happen the way we expect, it says, but that doesn't make the challenge of leading a productive life less interesting. We can, however, be more selective in the challenges we take up.

Nahien Hoti

har chand meri quvvat-e guftaar hai mahbuus
khaamosh magar tab'-e khud aara nahien hoti

Although my power of speech
is held captive,

silence is not understood
for what it really is.

maa'muura-e ehsaas mein hai hashar sa barpa
insaan ki tazlil gavaara nahien hoti

A multitude of feelings—
it looks like the chaos of doomsday—
but it is difficult for me to accept
the abasement of a human being.

naalaan huun main bedaari-e ehsaas ke haathon
duniya mere afkaar ki duniya nahien hoti

I am crying
while being swept away
by my self-awareness.
The world that I create
is not the world
that represents my thoughts.

begaana sifat jaadah-e manzil se guzar ja
har chiiz saza vaar-e nazzaara nahien hoti

Without any reservation
follow the path to your destination.
Every little indiscretion
does not deserve punishment.

fitrat ki mashiyyat bhi bari chiiz hai lekin
fitrat kabhi be-bas ka sahaara nahien hoti

Nature's bounty is a great gift,
but it does not become
the support system of a helpless human.

Eyes

Urdu poetry celebrates the beloved in many ways. The traditional approach is to shower praise on her curled black tresses, rose-like lips, lustrous cheeks, and, of course, deep black or blue eyes that bear a comparison to the depths of the ocean. In this ghazal, Sahir says that eyes are 'like a dewdrop, or a blaze, or a whirlwind'. Eyes reveal our personality. Among other things, eyes are the medium and kingpins of love. Words can be contrived, but the eyes always reveal the truth. They make or break us as human beings.

Aankhein

har tarah ke jazbaat ka ai'laan hain aankhein
shabnam kabhi sho'la kabhi tufaan hain aankhein

Eyes reflect and broadcast
our aspirations.
They are sometimes like a dewdrop,
or a blaze, or a whirlwind.

aankhon se bari koi taraazu nahien hoti
tulta hai bashar jis mein voh miizaan hain aankhein

There is no bigger measure than the eyes.
They are the gauge
of the worth of a human being.

aankhein hi milaati hain zamaane mein dilon ko
anjaan hain ham-tum agar anjaan hain aankhein

Eyes bring hearts together.
We are strangers if our eyes
have not shared glances.

lab kuchh bhi kahein is se haqiiqat nahien khulti
insaan ke sach jhuut ki pahchaan hain aankhein

Lips can speak
but the words do not reveal the truth.
The reality of a human
is seen through the eyes.

aankhein n jhukein teri kisi ghair ke aage
duniya mein bari chiiz meri jaan hain aankhein

Do not lower your eyes
in front of a stranger.
The way we use our eyes
in the world is a big deal,
my love!

Even Today

This ghazal reveals the same dissatisfaction that the poet had conveyed
in *'Chhabiis Janvari'* (see Chapter 1). We got our freedom but our
destiny has not changed. There is still injustice, and life is not easy for
most people. Though many brave souls gave up their lives to secure
the country's freedom, those who (presumably) collaborated with the
foreign power are still preaching. Their words are hollow because they
have nothing to say about the issues that are most important for
people—such as jobs, economic security, and social justice. There is
a jab at 'pompous gods' in the last couplet, a signature that identifies
Sahir as a progressive poet.

Aaj Bhi Hai

har qadam marhala-e daar o saliib aaj bhi hai
jo kabhi tha vohi insaan ka nasiib aaj bhi hai

Each step reminds us
how close we are to the places
where bodies are hung.
Man's destiny is the same
even today.

jagmagaate hain ufaq par y sitaare lekin
raasta manzil-e hasti ka muhiib aaj bhi hai

Stars in the sky shine but
the path of life is dreadful
even today.

sar-e maqtal jinhein jaana tha voh ja bhi pahunche
sar-e mimbar koi mohtaat khatiib aaj bhi hai

Those destined
for slaughterhouses
have finally arrived.
But the reverent preacher
standing behind the lectern
is preaching even today.

ahl-e daanish ne jise amr-e musallum maana
ahl-e dil ke liye voh baat a'jiib aaj bhi hai

What the wise
consider to be universally true
the tender-hearted find rather strange
even today.

y teri yaad hai ya meri aziyat koshi
ek nashtar sa rag-e jaan ke qariib aaj bhi hai

Is this a memory of you
or a way to torture me?
I find something like a lancet
sitting near my jugular even today.

kaun jaane y tera shaa'yir-e aashufta mizaj
kitne maghruur khudaaon ka raqiib aaj bhi hai

Few know
that this distraction-prone poet of yours
is a rival to many pompous gods even today.

Come Close to Me

This is an exquisite romantic ghazal of four couplets, sung by Mohammad Rafi for the 1977 movie *Amaanat*, and stylistically, it steals the reader's heart. The tone is conversational or invitational. The lover is asking the beloved to come up to him and he gives all kinds of reasons: By coming up to me, you will make this night memorable; I will be able to touch you, something I always yearned for; my body is simultaneously overwhelmed by hot and cold flames; there is a partnership for life that could be sustained only by your coming up to me ... Bravo!

Qariib Aa Jaao

duur rah kar n karo baat qariib aa jaao
yaad rah jaaye gi y raat qariib aa jaao

Don't talk to me
when you are standing apart.
The memory of this night shall live.
Come up to me!

ek muddat se tamanna thi tumhein chhune ki
aaj bas mein nahien jazbaat qairiib aa jaao

For a very long time
I yearned to touch you.
Today, my craving for you
is beyond my control.
Come up to me!

sard jhonkon se bharakte hain badan mein sho'ale
jaan le legi y barsaat qariib aa jaao

Cold flames,
hot flames engulf my body.
This downpour will end my life.
Come up to me!

is qadar ham se jhijakne ki zaruurat kya hai
zindagi bhar ka hai ab saath qariib aa jaao

There is no need to be so diffident.
We have a partnership for life.
Come up to me!

I Saw It

This ghazal gained great popularity for the simplicity and beauty of its couplets. Blaming the heart for love's complications is an old device. Several other poets have tried to pinpoint the conflict between meeting the demands of making a living and sustaining a loving relationship. Sahir has ploughed this ground before.

Dekha To Tha

dekha to tha yuun hi kisi ghaflat shi'aar ne
divaana kar diya dile-e be ikhtiyaar ne

Even someone
who was not paying attention saw it—
my unrestrained heart was responsible
for my madness.

ai aarzu ke dhundhle kharaabo javaab do
phir kis ki yaad aayi thi mujh ko pukaar ne

I want an answer
from the foggy spoilers
of my wishes and dreams—

whose voice was it
that called my name?

tujh ko khabar nahien magar ik saada lauh ko
barbaad kar diya tere do din ke pyaar ne

You may not know it
but a simpleton was ruined
by your short-lived love!

main aur tum se tark-e mohabbat ki aarzu
divaana kar diya hai gham-e rozgaar ne

Can I even entertain
the thought of giving up
loving you?
But please do realize
I've lost my good sense
in the pain of making a living.

ab ai dil-e tabaah tera kya khayaal hai
ham to chale the kaakul-e giiti sanvaarne

O my ruined heart,
what do you think
of the mess we are in?
Remember, we set off
with the aim of decorating
the tresses of life.

Life Up Close

This ghazal, partially used for the 1975 movie *Ek Mahal Ho Sapnon Ka* and sung by Kishore Kumar, starts like a typical romantic melody with a theme that Sahir has touched upon in many poems: a poor man loses his love because of his poverty. But the last four couplets, not used for the film song, are remarkable for the newness of topics and profundity of their lyricism. Notice the imagery of prophets calling from their bloodied crosses, of patients arguing with their caregivers, of a slaughterhouse that can be reached only from the beloved's alley, or that you are forced to accept your rival as your companion!

Dekha Hai Zindagi Ko

dekha hai zindagi ko kuchh itna qariib se
chehre tamaam lagne lage hain a'jiib se

When I saw life up close,
the faces of people looked
quite strange to me.

kahne ko dil ki baat jinhein dhuundhte the ham
mahfil mein aa gaye hain voh apne nasiib se

The one person,
I was looking for
to share what was in my heart,
has just entered the party.
My good luck!

niilaam ho raha tha kisi naazniin ka pyaar
qiimat nahien chukaayi gayi ik gariib se

When a delicate maiden's love
was being auctioned,
the poor man had no money
in his pocket to make a bid.

teri vafa ki laash p la main hi daal duun
resham ka y kafan jo mila hai raqiib se

Please allow me
to cover the dead body

of your faithfulness
with the silken shroud
that my rival has gifted to you.

ai ruuh-e a'sr jaag kahaan so rahi hai tu
aavaaz de rahe hain payamber saliib se

O spirit of the times,
you have fallen asleep.
Prophets are calling
from their bloodied crosses.

is rengti hayaat ka kab tak uthaayein baar
bimaar ab ulajhne lage hain tabiib se

How long have we to carry
the burden of this slithering life?
Patients are now arguing
with their caregivers.

har gaam par hai majm'a-e u'shshaaq muntazir
maqtal ki raah milti hai kuu-e habiib se

Every step of the way
there is a crowd of lovers,
just waiting.
But the slaughterhouse
can be reached
only from the beloved's alley.

is tarah zandagi ne diya hai hamaara saath
jaise koi nibaah raha ho raqiib se

Life has given us
the comfort of a companion
in the same way

as if someone was forced
to spend his time
with his rival.

Something Happens ...

This remarkable ghazal written for the 1965 film *Waqt* was beautifully sung by Asha Bhosle. It is an out-and-out sensory experience, a treat for the ears, eyes, brain, and heart.

Aa Jaata Hai

chehre p khushi aa jaati hai aankhon mein suruur aa jaata hai
jab tum mujhe apna kahte ho apne p ghuruur aa jaata hai

Euphoric bliss covers my face
and my eyes are filled with a joyous glitter.
When you tell me 'you are mine'
my delight knows no bounds.

tum husn ki khud ik duniya ho shaayad y tumhein maa'luum nahien
mahfil mein tumhaare aane se har chiiz p nuur aa jaata hai

You are the heavenly body of beauty
and probably you don't know it.
When you enter the congregation,
everything lights up.

ham paas se tum ko kya dekhein tum jab bhi muqabil hote ho
betaab nigaahon ke aage pardah sa zaruur aa jaata hai

When we are standing face-to-face
I can't just look at you.
A curtain falls over my restless eyes.

jab tum se muhabbat ki ham ne tab ja ke kahin y raaz khula
marne ka saliiqa aate hi jiine ka shu'uur aa jaata hai

I got to know this secret
when I fell in love with you.
Awareness of what it means to be alive
dawned on me
when I learnt the art of dying gracefully.

I Have Doused the Flames of Love

Written like a traditional ghazal, this one depicts a lover's dilemma: of coping with the realities of life after his love affair has finally come to an end. Where should he go when 'the hamlets of hope are now in ruins'? What will happen if the two of them meet again? The poet has a specific suggestion on how to avoid such an unsavoury situation. There is a life to be lived even after love has flown the coop.

Bujha Diye Hain

bhuja diye hain khud apne haathon mohabbaton ke diye jala ke
meri vafa ne ujaar di hain ummiid ki bastiyaan basa ke

I lit the candles of love
but now I have doused them with my own hands.
The hamlets of hope are now in ruins,
thanks to my faithfulness.

tujhe bhula dein ge apne dil se y faisla to kiya hai lekin
n dil ko maa'luum hai n ham ko jiyein ge kaise tujhe bhula ke

I have decided to remove you
from my heart.
But how will I live?
Neither my heart nor I know
anything about it.

kabhi milein ge jo raaste mein to munh phira kar palat parein ge
kahin sunein ge jo naam tera to chup rahein gein sar jhuka ke

If by chance we meet again,
we shall look at each other and then
turn our faces away.
If I hear your name somewhere
I will bow my head down and stay silent.

n sochne par bhi sochta huun k zindagaani mein kya rahega
teri tamanna ko dafn kar ke tere khayaalon se duur ja ke

Though I don't want to think about it,
I keep wondering,
what shall become of my life—
if I buried my desire for you
and stopped thinking about you?

The Heart After All

Another popular ghazal from the 1963 movie *Dil Hi To Hai*, this was
sung by Mukesh in his unique voice. Not included in the song was the
most significant couplet:

jazbaat bhi hindu hote hain chaahat bhi musalmaan hoti hai
duniya ka ishaara tha lekin samjha n ishara dil hi to hai

Feelings can be labelled Hindu,
love can be called Muslim.
The world was sending these signals,
but the heart didn't get it—
it was the heart after all.

Here is the rest of the ghazal:

Dil Hi To Hai

bhuule se mohabbat kar baitha nadaan tha bechara dil hi to hai
har dil se khata ho jaati hai bigro n khudaara dil hi to hai

Falling in love was a mistake—
the work of my innocent and pitiable heart!
The heart is capable of making a mistake.
Don't get upset for god's sake—
it is the heart after all.

is tarah nigahein mat phero aisa n ho dharkan ruk jaaye
siine mein koi patthar to nahien ehsaas ka mara dil hi to hai

Don't turn your eyes away from me.
I might stop breathing!
There is no stone in my chest—
the victim of my suffering is the heart after all.

bedaad garon ki thokar se sab khwaab suhaane chuur hue
ab dil ka sahara gham hi to hai ab gham ka sahara dil hi to hai

Knocked down by oppressors
my alluring dreams shattered.
My sorrows are now nursing my heart
and my heart is being nursed by my woes.

Let Us Ask

Sahir had the uncanny ability to write a ghazal that read beautifully
and had great lyrical quality—but had little to say in terms of content.
This one is an example. Read it, enjoy it while it lasts—there is nothing
more to it.

Puuchhte Chalo

ab aayein ya n aayein idhar puuchhte chalo
kya chahti hai unki nazar puuchhte chalo

Now, she may or may not come.
Let us ask.

231

What do her eyes wish?
Let us ask.

ham se agar hai tark-e ta'lluq to kya hua
yaaro koi to un ki khabar puucchte chalo

It doesn't matter that
our relations have come to an end.
But, friends, what about her well-being?
Let us ask.

jo khud ko kah rahe hain k manzil shanaas hain
un ko bhi kya khabar hai magar puucchte chalo

There are those
who know where they are going.
But they may not know it all.
Let us ask.

kis manzil-e muraad ki jaanib ravaan hain ham
ae rah ravaan-e khaak basar puuchhte chalo

What is the destination
of our soul's journey?
Think of travellers living in dust!
Let us ask.

The Right Offering

If a ghazal is to be judged by the sheer abundance of romanticism, then
this one takes the prize. Though the words are simple, the emotions are
deep: Love is an unconditional offering. If your heart is deeply stirred
after reading this ghazal, then the poet clearly achieved his objective.

Kya Pesh Karuun

apna dil pesh karuun apni vafa pesh karuun
kuchh samajh mein nahien aata tujhe kya pesh karuun

Should I offer
my heart or my fidelity?
I don't know
what's the right offering.

tere milne ki khushi mein koi naghma chheruun
ya tere dard-e judaai ka gila pesh karuun

Would you like me to sing
a melody to celebrate our meeting?
Or should I offer a lamentation
about the pain of our separation?

mere khwaabon mein bhi tu mere khayaalon mein bhi tu
kaun si chiiz tujhe tujh se juda pesh karuun

You live in my dreams
as well as in my thoughts.
What can I offer
that you might consider special?

jo tire dil ko lubhaae vo ada mujh mein nahien
kyun n tujh ko koi teri hi ada pesh karuun

What pleases you
is not within the range
of my abilities.
Would it be right
if I offer you
one of your own
flirtatious moves?

Take It with You

This ghazal was written for the 1976 movie *Laila Majnun* and sung by Mohammad Rafi. The love between the two title characters ended in

great tragedy. The lyrics describe the moments of their parting. The
lover has already given her all he had to give. Now he has only words
and prayers left.

Saath Liye Ja

barbaad-e mohabbat ki dua saath liye ja
tuuta hua iqrar-e vafa saath liye ja

Take the prayers
of one
who has been ruined in love.
Take with you
the broken affirmations
of fidelity.

ik dil tha jo pahle hi tujhe saunp diya tha
y jaan bhi ai jaan-e ada saath liye ja

I had one heart
that I have already gifted you.
Take with you
the breath of my body
as a plaything.

tapti hui raahon se tujhe aanch n pahunche
divaanon ke ashkon ki ghata saath liye ja

I don't want
any harm done to you
by the heat of life's passages.
Take with you
the cloudy tears
of your maniacal lovers.

shaamil hai mera khuun-e jigar teri henna mein
y kam ho to ab khuun-e vafa saath liye ja

Your henna contains
the blood of my heart.
If you wish,
take with you
the blood of infidelities.

ham jurm-e mohabbat ki saza paaenge tanha
jo tujh se hui ho vo khata saath liye ja

I would suffer
the punishment
for loving you
on my own.
If you did anything wrong,
take that crime with you
when you leave.

We

This ghazal is a mixture of disappointment and hope. All the major
progressive poets had grand visions of a world of plenty enjoyed by
all. Sahir, while conceding that things have not gone according to the
plan, reminds you that all is not lost, as some progress has been made.

Ham

bharka rahe hain aag lab-e naghma gar se ham
khaamosh kya rahenge zamaane ke dar se ham

We are fanning
the fury of the fire
with help
from the lips of the lyricist.
Why should we be afraid
of the time and circumstances
in which we live?

kuchh aur barh gae jo andhere to kya hua
maayuus to nahien hain tulu-e sahar se ham

It doesn't matter
that darkness has spread
so fast.
We are hopeful
that the sun will rise
when the morning comes.

le de ke apne paas faqat ik nazar to hai
kyun dekhein zindagi ko kisi ki nazar se ham

An inventory
of what we are left with
reveals nothing but our dreams.
Why should we look at life
with the eyes of those
who are not our friends?

maana k is zamiin ko n gulzaar kar sake
kuchh khaar kam to kar gae guzre jidhar se ham

Agreed
that we failed to make this world
a flourishing garden of hope.
But we did remove some thorns
from the paths that we traversed.

I Felt Like Crying

Tragedy was at its prime in Hindi cinema during the 1950s and 1960s. Lost love and downhearted heroes singing lonesome songs was the norm. Class differences killed profound love affairs. Family honour demanded lovers to sacrifice their love for each other. These were themes that were repeated film after film. Sahir was a reliable medium to deliver on such situations. This ghazal, which was sung by Mohammad Rafi for the 1961 movie *Hum Dono*, is a good example. The last couplet is the most memorable.

Rona Aaya

kabhi khud p kabhi halaat p rona aaya
baat nikli to har ik baat p rona aaya

I cried for myself at times,
and sometimes at my circumstances.
When things became public,
at every bit of gossip.

ham to samjhe the k ham bhuul gae hain unko
kya hua aaj ye kis baat p rona aaya

I had thought
that I had forgotten her.
I don't know what happened today
that I snapped at something so small.

kis liye jiite hain ham kis ke liye marte hain
baarha aise savalaat p rona aaya

Why do we live?
For whom do we give away
our life?
These questions
have tortured me.

kaun rota hai kisi ki khatir ai dost
sab ko apni hi kisi baat p rona aaya

My friend,
no one cries
for the sake of another.
Everyone cries
for something
that touches them
deeply.

Walked Away

Another ghazal from the film *Hum Dono*, also sung by Mohammad Rafi, this one is unique for its definitional tenor. The poet is defining a character who has seen the ups and downs of life without feeling much remorse about it. The words are simple, but there is a magic in the way they unfold. Worries bug you, but why not blow them away in smoke? Bad things happen, but why not celebrate them? What is the purpose of remembering friends you have lost? Joys and sorrows follow in quick succession, but why not keep your heart steady?

Chala Gaya

main zindagi ka saath nibhata chala gaya
har fikr ko dhuen mein uraata chala gaya

I walked
shoulder to shoulder with life.
I puffed away
every worry and every concern.

barbaadiyon ka sog manana fazuul tha
barbaadiyon ka jashn manata chala gaya

It was futile to feel sorry
for all kinds of ruinations.
I did the odd thing
and celebrated everything
that life tore down.

jo mil gaya usi ko muqaddar samajh liya
jo kho gaya main us ko bhulata chala gaya

I treated friends and companions
as guardians of my fate.

And those that I lost in the process
I slowly tried to forget.

gham aur khushi mein farq mahsuus ho jahaan
main dil ko us maqaam p laata chala gaya

In a world
where you can't feel
any difference between
joy and sadness,
I purposefully trained
my heart
to be rightfully in that place.

4
Bhajans
One Above, One Below

Come, meet me, Shyaam,
my dusky, blue-tinged lover.
Radha is feeling lost in Brij.
Oh! Radha is wandering adrift.
Come, Krishna, meet me.

—'Come, Meet Me'

Sahir was a staunch secularist and therefore he always spoke against religious fanaticism and separatism. He never associated himself with narrow interpretations that used religion as a dividing factor among people. There is no evidence that he practised any religion. Yet, as Gopi Chand Narang points out, Sahir wrote some of the best bhajans ever written for Hindi cinema. The bhajan genre, with its emphasis on the spiritual or religious, is very different from the ghazal and other forms of Urdu poetry. Also, knowledge of dialects like Braj Bhasha, Oudhi, and Rajasthani is also needed, along with a fairly good understanding of bhajans written by great seers and saints like Sur Das, Tulsi Das, and Mira Bai. Narang explains:

In India, bhakti has two major streams—Krishna bhakti and Rama bhakti. Both are based on feelings of love and devotion. In Krishna-bhakti there is an added facet of romance, coupled with songs and dances. Rama is the symbol of duty, sacrifice, good deeds, and morality. Sahir wrote bhajans that captured both these traditions and moods … [He] also wrote bhajans that were quite separate from the Krishna and Rama traditions. The focus of these bhajans was human brotherhood, religious tolerance, and even personal enlightenment based on the mastery of one's mind, as in *Tero Man Darpan Kahlaaye* (The mind is the mirror of one's inner self).[1]

Even if all is forgotten, Sahir will be remembered for his powerful statement of religious unity: '*Allah tero naam, Ishwar tero naam, sab ko sanmati de Bhagwaan.*' Allah and Ishwar are your names. O Lord, give the gift of rightful thinking to all. Narang says in his conclusion:

> The world of bhajan poetry can be vast and limited. It is wide because spirituality and ethics are like the horizon where we meet as human beings and we reflect on our births (Why am I here?) and deaths (Where do I go when I die?). It can be limited because a bhajan appeals to one's belief system based on one's concept of unity and non-duality, or oneness with God. Sahir's great achievement was that he created great poetry together with great lyricism and musicality, without losing the overarching purpose, which was to create a certain mood, a certain feeling of oneness. Whether it was Krishna Leela, Ishwar–Allah, Ram–Raheem, Krishna–Kareem, Kabir–Nanak, Sahir shaped his offerings in a creative mould that would be remembered for ages.[2]

Bhajan—a genre that draws inspiration from the life stories and special attributes of Hindu gods and goddesses—has great attraction for a very large segment of the population. Much of this stems from the way it is sung, so as to create a devotional state of mind, often boosting one's spirit, akin to an out-of-body experience in which the listener forgets the worries and anxieties of day-to-day life. Sahir, as a devout Marxist, does not seem to be an ideal candidate to be a bhajan writer, but it is to his credit that he made a special effort to gain skills and embrace a spiritual temperament suited to writing some of the finest bhajans that Hindi cinema has offered over decades of its existence.

---

[1] Gopi Chand Narang, '*Sahir Ludhianvi Aur Bhajan Ki Maanuyat*', URDU Quarterly Magazine, 2–4, 2013: 16.

[2] Narang, '*Sahir Ludhianvi Aur Bhajan Ki Maanuyat*', 16.

Allah and Ishwar are Your Names

This bhajan, written in true Gandhian spirit, is a marvellous piece of writing. It celebrates the core of humanness that transcends all religious denominations. In a country where countless numbers of people died at the very dawn of freedom because of bigotry and divisiveness—and as countless numbers have died since—the message of communal harmony is of paramount importance. Sahir wrote a bhajan that reminds people of the oneness of god, though the customs of worship might differ from one faith to another.

Allah and Ishwar are your names.
O Lord, give the gift of right thinking to all!

May this land sustain its beauty.
May the cool sunshine of love stay forever.
May everyone get an offering of truth.
Lord, give the gift of right thinking to all.

Let the sindoor in the parting of the hair
continue to radiate a marital relationship.
Keep the hope alive for mothers and sisters.
Don't let any soul wander without a body.
Lord, give the gift of right thinking to all!
Allah and Ishwar are your names.

O the Saviour of the whole universe—
a source of strength for the weak.
Give wisdom to the powerful.
Lord, give the gift of right thinking to all!

Allah and Ishwar are your names.

Allah Tero Naam, Ishwar Tero Naam

Allah tero naam Ishwar tero naam
sabko sanmati de Bhagwaan

is dharti ka ruup n ujre
pyaar ki thandi dhuup n ujre
sab ko mile sach ka vardaan
sab ko sanmati de Bhagwaan

maangon ka sindhuur n chhuute
maan bahnon ki aas n tuute
deh bina daata
bhatke n praan
sabko sanmati de Bhagwaan
Allah tero naam
Ishwar tero naam

o saare jag ke rakhvaale
nirbal ko bal dene vaale
balvaano ko de de gyaan
sabko sanmati de Bhagwaan

Allah tero naam
Ishwar tero naam

Those Who Think of You

This bhajan reinforces the idea that meditation on the divine name, without any motive or expectation, offered from the sincerity of one's heart, is itself a great reward. There is no need to ask for anything because nothing is hidden from the divine, even to our deepest desires. The greatest gift of this kind of meditation is not material. It is peace of mind and a state of tranquillity.

Almighty
those who think of your name
get peace and serenity in return.

If you are pleased, O Beneficent,
the riches of life are the reward.
The seeker gains contentment
from your name.

Those who meditate on your name
get peace and serenity in return.

You are beneficent,
you are omniscient.
If you are pleased
every difficult task becomes easy.
Life is rich.
Your name gives happiness.
Those who meditate on your name
reap rich rewards.
Your name brings peace.

If you are pleased
my empty courtyard
will be full of happiness.
My withered marriage
will blossom.
My life will be filled with sweetness.
Life will be rich,
as your name brings happiness.
Those who meditate on your name
reap rich rewards.
Your name brings peace.

Prabhu Tero Naam

Prabhu tero naam
jo dhyaaye phal paaye
sukh laaye tero naam

teri daya ho jaaye to daata
jiivan dhan mil jaaye mil jaaye
mil jaaye, sukh daaye tero naam
jo dhyaaye phal paaye
sukh daaye tero naam

tu daani tu antaryaami
teri kripaa ho jaaye to swaami
har bigri ban jaaye
jiivan dhan mil jaaye mil jaaye
mil jaaye, sukh daaye tero naam
jo dhyaaye phal paaye
sukh laaye tero naam

bas jaaye mora suuna angna
khil jaaye murjhaayaa kangna
jiivan mein ras laaye
jiivan dhan mil jaaye mil jaaye
mil jaaye sukh laaye tero naam
jo dhyaaye phal paaye
sukh laaye tero naam

The Self is the Mirror

If there is one binding idea that you find in scriptures from different faiths, it is the importance of the self (sometimes written as 'Self'). In Hindu theology, it is the bridge between the personal self (*atma*) and the Divine Self (*parmatma*). The central theme of this bhajan, of the self as a mirror, is a very powerful idea. It is an invitation for introspection, of evaluating our mental and emotional strengths and weaknesses. Inner awareness equals inner illumination, because without any external help we are able to judge our good and bad actions. Once we know who we really are, many pathways to self-improvement open for us.

Your Self is called the mirror.
Good deeds and bad deeds,
it sees and it reflects them all.

The Self is the deity, the Self is Ishwar,
there is nothing bigger than the Self.
The Self is the lighthouse.
When it spreads its light

the whole world is illuminated.
On the clear surface of the Self,
O living being,
make sure dust doesn't gather.
Your Self is called the mirror.
Good deeds and bad deeds,
it sees and it reflects them all.

The buds of happiness,
the thorns of suffering,
the Self is the foundation of all.
Nothing is hidden from the Self.
The Self has a thousand eyes.
You can run away from the world,
but you can't run away from the Self.
Your Self is called the mirror.
Good deeds and bad deeds
it sees and it reflects them all.

The wealth of the body is like a passing shadow.
The Self's treasure is invaluable.
Because of your fascination for the material body,
do not grind the wealth of the Self into dirt.
The one who forgets the Self's merit
will waste the gift this life brings.
Your Self is called the mirror.
Good deeds and bad deeds
it sees and it reflects them all.

Tora Man Darpan Kehlaaye

tora man darpan kahlaaye
bhale bure saare karmon ko
dekhe aur dikhaaye

man hi devta, man hi Ishwar, man se bada n koe
man ujiyaara jab jab phaile jag ujiyaaraa hoe

is ujle darpan par praani dhuul n jamne paaye
tora man darpan kahlaaye
bhale bure saare karmon ko
dekhe aur dikhaaye
tora man darpan kahlaaye

sukh ki kaliyaan dukh ke kaante man sabkaa aadhaar
man se koyi baat chhupe n man ke nain hazaar
jag se chaahe bhaag le koi man se bhaag n paaye
tora man darpan kahlaaye
bhale bure saare karmon ko
dekhe aur dikhaaye
tora man darpan kahlaaye

tan ki daulat dhalti chhaaya man ka dhan anmol
tan ke kaaran man ke dhan ko mat maati mein raund
man ki qadar bhulaanevaala viiraan janam ganvaaye
tora man darpan kahlaaye
bhale bure saare karmon ko,
dekhe aur dikhaaye
tora man darpan kahlaaye

Come, Meet Me

This is a Krishna-bhakti bhajan and is filled with emotions of love and reverence. It captures Radha's feeling as she wanders the streets of Brindaban in search of her lover, Shyaam (Lord Krishna). Radha in this case is the metaphor for all individual souls who are wandering without the loving care of the Lord, the Universal Lover. There is an urgency in the words that acts as a motivating force for the devotee's spirit. There can be no peace of mind without Shyaam's loving embrace. And it must happen now.

Come, meet me, Shyaam,
my dusky, blue-tinged lover, come, meet me!

Lonely Radha is wandering adrift and is lost in Brij.
The heart has no comfort without you in the streets
of Brindaban.
There is talk of you every day.
Oh, how unfortunate are my restless eyes!
If this is the state of my mind now
what will happen to me in the days to come?
Lonely Radha is wandering adrift in Brij
with tears in her eyes.
Come, Kanha, meet me!

Why didn't you play your flute today?
Why didn't you dance today with my friends?
Which hamlet did you decide to go to,
leaving my courtyard?
Lonely Radha is wandering adrift and is lost in Brij.
Come, Krishna, meet me!

Without any word from you, O Mohan,
this girl from Brij
is going crazy crying.
Come and console me and show me your face.
O great dancer, my dusky lover,
Radha is feeling lost in Brij.
O Radha is wandering adrift and is lost in Brij.
Come Krishna, meet me.

Aan Milo

Aan milo aan milo Shyam saanvare aan milo

Brij mein akeli Raadhe khoyi khoyi phire
Brindaban ki galiyon mein tum bin jiyara na laage
nis din tumri baat nihaare vyaakul nain abhaage
ab han aisi disha hai mann ki ka hui hai phir aage
Brij mein akeli Raadhe royi royi phire
o Kanha aan milo

aaj na kaahe Jamuna tere murli madhur bajaayi
aaj na kaahe sakhiyon ke sang hil mil raas rachaayi
hamra aangan chhor ke tohe kaun nagariya bhaaii re
Brij mein akeli Raadhe khooii khooii phire
o Kanha aan milo

ajhun jo n bheje re Mohan taine koyi khabariyaa
ho jaaii hai y Brij ki baala ro ro kar baanvariya
dhiir bandha ja mukh dikhla ja nat naagar saanvariya re
Brij mein akeli Raadhe khooii khooii phire
o Kanha aan milo

Take Me in Your Arms

Another very beautiful Krishna-bhakti bhajan that touches the summits of devotional romanticism, in this, only union with the Lord can bring solace to Radha's soul. 'Take me into your arms, O my lover,' she pleads. Nothing else will calm the body's pain and douse the fire that slowly burns from a state of separation. It is absolute union, of fusing body and soul, that will quench the eternal thirst. There is no substitute for this union, which must happen now, without any further wait.

After suffering repeated bouts of separation
Radha lost her patience and one day
she approached her lover and proclaimed:

Take me in your arms, O my lover.
Make my life meaningful.
My heart's pain and my body's fire—
allow them to cool down.
They have been awake for ages—
my unfortunate eyes.
My heart finds no comfort anywhere.
It does not see any repose ahead.

Sufferings are running after me,
chasing me.

Without you the world looks
rather desolate to me.
O my lover, my nectar.
My dusky lover.
Let there be a downpour of
the sweet rain of love
that floods the whole world.

Take me in your arms, O my lover.
Make my life meaningful.

Make me your own.
Make me your own by clutching my hand.
I am your servant life after life.
Quench my thirst.
Heart-stealer, just quench my thirst.
My thirst is deep,
my body and soul are thirsty.
My lover, my nectar.
Take me in your arms, O my lover.
Make my life meaningful.
My heart's pain and my body's fire—
allow them to cool down.

Aaj Sajan Mohe Ang Lagaa Lo

birhaa ke dukhre sah sah kar jab Raadhe besudh ho li
to ik din apne manmohan se ja kar yuun boli

aaj sajan mohe ang lagaalo
janam safal ho jaaye
hriday ki piira deh ki agni
sab shiital ho jaaye

kaii yug se hain jaage
more nain abhaage

kahiin jiyaa nahien laage bin tore
sukh dekhe nahien aage

dukh piichhe piichhe bhaage
jag suuna suuna laage bin tore
prem sudha,
moray saanvariyaa
saanvariyaa
prem sudha itni barsa do
jag jal thal ho jaaye

aaj sajan mohe ang lagaalo
janam safal ho jaaye

mohe apnaa banaalo
mohe apnaa banaalo mori baanh pakar
main huun janam janam ki daasi
mohe apna banaalo mori baanh pakar
main huun janam janam ki daasi
meri pyaas bujha do
manhar giridhar pyaas bujha do
manhar giridhar pyaas bujha do
manhar giridhar
main huun antarghat tak pyaasi
prem sudha

aaj sajan mohe ang lagaalo
janam safal ho jaaye
hriday ki piiraa deh ki agni
sab shiital ho jaaye

Whenever Rama Took Birth

This is a bhajan of Rama bhakti, a lamentation on how humans have failed in every age to recognize the true greatness of Rama, the exemplar of goodness. Why is he exiled every time he reincarnates?

The reason is not too difficult to find. As human beings, we are too obsessed with greed and other weaknesses to pay attention, and if Rama has to suffer while roaming the forests, we are comfortable with that. Lord Rama is the symbol of a perfect human being; he is the repository of moral goodness. It is our blindness that we are not able to recognize him when he comes to live among us and to show us the right path of noble living, which is consistent with the aspirations of our spirit.

The world, contaminated by lust, anger, and greed,
has not been the right place.
Whenever Rama incarnated, he was given exile.

The practice that originated in Satyuga
has survived until the days of Kalyuga.
When he lost everything that belonged to him,
only then Rama emerged victorious.
Yugas pass on but this history has not changed.
Whenever Rama incarnated, he was given exile.

Leaving his glorious palaces
to roam the forests.
For the contentment of others,
placing himself in the midst of jeopardy.
This is the essence of Rama's story.
Do you believe it now?
Whenever Rama incarnated, he was given exile.

Rama came to this world in every yuga.
But who recognized him?
Rama was worshipped,
but no one understood his message.
Both earth and sky grew old looking at this.
Whenever Rama incarnated, he was given exile.

Jab Jab Ram Ne Janam Liya

kaam krodh aur lobh ka maaraa
jagat n aaya raas
jab jab Ram ne janm liya
tab tab paaya banvaas

Kalyug tak chalti aayee hai
Satyug ki yeh riit
Kalyug tak chalti aayee hai
Satyug ki yeh riit
sab kuchh haar chuke jab apna
tab ho Ram ki jiit
jug badle par badal n paaya
ab tak yeh itihaas
jab jab Ram ne janam liya
tab tab paaya banvaas

chhod ke apne mahal do mahle
jungle jungle phirna
chhod ke apne mahal do mahle
jungle jungle phirna
auron ke sukh chain ki khaatir
dukh sankat mein ghirna
hai yahi Ram ke lekh ki rekha
aa gaya ab vishvaas
jab jab Ram ne janam liya
tab tab paaya banvaas

Ram har ek yug mein aaye
par kaun unhe pehchana
Ram har ek yug mein aaye
par kaun unhe pehchana
Ram ki puuja ki jag ne
par Ram ka arth n jaana

takte takte buurhe ho gaye
dharti aur aakaash

jab jab Ram ne janam liya
tab tab paaya banvaas
kaam krodh aur lobh ka maaraa
jagat n aaya raas
jab jab Ram ne janam liya
tab tab paaya banvaas

Ganga

There is no river more sacred than the Ganga, the abode of the goddess for whom it is named. It is believed that bathing in the Ganga absolves sins and prepares one for the attainment of moksha. The river, in its journey of around 1,500 miles, passes by places like Haridwar and Varanasi that are important centres of pilgrimage. Historically, many ancient kingdoms flourished on the banks of the Ganga. The waters of this river support agriculture and other industries that provide livelihood to millions. A celebration of the Ganga, this bhajan combines thoughts and prayers that are expressions of the Hindu faith as well as commemoration of life in general.

Victory to Ganga!
Glory to Ganga!

Ganga,
While singing your praises,
the world falls to its knees.
You are our life's saviour.
You are the source of our salvation.
If we get your protection, O mother,
our life becomes meaningful.
Ganga,
your water has the sweetness of nectar.
Wave after wave the water flows.

Yuga after yuga, age after age,
our motherland has nourished
life with your bliss and grace.
Ganga,
your water has the sweetness of nectar.

From the far Himalayas you descend
singing pleasant songs,
bringing a message of happiness
from village to jungle.
Your silvery waters
flow for miles.
Ganga,
your water has the sweetness of nectar.

Scores of suns have risen and set,
Ganga, at your doorstep.
The swings and flourishes of your waters
tell the story of all yugas.
Without you, Ganga,
the story of India can't be written.
Ganga,
your water has the sweetness of nectar.

You have absorbed the triumphs and travails
that this earth has seen.
Whenever this country
was enchained
your waters shed tears.
Whenever we gained liberty
your banks smiled.
Ganga,
your water has the sweetness of nectar.

On your banks is resonating
the melody of new life.

You create a confluence of streams,
we do the same for our fields.
This is the same confluence
that brings hearts together.
Ganga,
your water has the sweetness of nectar.

Ganga

jai jai Gangay
har har Gangay

har har Gangay keh ke duniya
tere aage jhukti
tujhi se hum sab jiivan paayein
tujhi se paayein mukti
teri sharan miley to maiyya
janam safal ho jaaye
Ganga tera paani amrit
jhar jhar behta jaaye
yug yug se is desh ki dharti
tujh se jiivan paaye
Ganga tera paani amrit

duur Himalaya se tu aayii
giit suhaane gaati
basti basti jungle jungle
sukh sandesh sunaati
teri chaandi jaisi dhaara
miilon tak lehraaye
ganga tera paani amrit

kitne suraj ubhare duube
Ganga tere dvaare
yugon yugon ki katha sunnaayein
tere behte dhaare

tujh ko chhod ke Bharat ka
itihaas likhaa n jaaye
Ganga tera paani amrit

is dharti ka dukh sukh tu ne
apne biich samoyaa
jab jab desh ghulaam huaa hai
tera paani roya
jab jab hum azaad huye hain
tere tat muskaaye
Ganga tera paani amrit

jhar jhar behtaa jaaye
yug yug se is desh ki dharti
tujh se jiivan paaye
Ganga tera paani amrit

guunj rahi hai tere tat par
navjiivan ki sargam
tu nadiyon ka sangam karti
hum kheton ka sangam
yahi voh sangam hai jo
dil ka dil se mel karaaye
Ganga tera paani amrit
jhar jhar behta jaaye
yug yug se iss desh ki dharti
tujh se jiivan paaye
Ganga tera paani amrit

Why are You Anxious?

This is another beautiful bhajan of Rama bhakti. As human beings, we face one problem after another, one issue after another. But there is a solution that brings us salvation from worldly affairs: coming to Rama's door and seeking his blessings. This is a door that is always open. No one who comes here leaves disheartened. The Lord listens to our prayers and makes no judgements. If we pray with utmost sincerity, we will surely get what we want.

Why are you anxious?
There are millions of beings
who are needy and suffering.
They attain salvation
at Rama's doors with his blessings
and grace.

His doors are never closed.
Yugas come and go.
Those who lost at others' gates
were victorious at this one.
Millions who were fallen and disgraced
showed their remorse,
and came away redeemed
from Rama's doors.
Why are you anxious?

We are the foolish ones who mess up.
Rama sets things right.
Whether it is Mahananda or Ahilya,
he delivers them all to heaven.
Even the pebble that his feet graze
ends up showing the path.
At Rama's doors,
why are you anxious?

He does not test anyone's knowledge.
No questions about merits and shortcomings.
No judgements whatsoever.
Only that devotee is dear to the Lord
who desires and understands his message.
The one who approaches with full faith
takes away a lot.

At Rama's doors,
Why are you anxious?

Tora Manva Kyun Ghabraaye Re

tora manva kyun ghabraaye re
laakh diin dukhiyaare saare
jag mein mukti paayein
he Raam ji ke dvaar se

band huaa y dvaar kabhi n
yug kitne hi biite
sab dvaaron par haarne vaale
is dvaare par jiite
laakhon patit laakhon pachhtaaye
paavan hokar aaye re
Raam ji ke dvaar se
tora manva kyun ghabraaye re

laakh diin dukhiyaare praani
jag mein mukti paaye
he Raam ji ke dvaar se

ham muurakh jo kaaj bigaare
Raam vo kaaj sanvaare
Raam vo kaaj sanvaare
ho Mahananda ho ke Ahilya
sab ko paar utaare
sab ko paar utaare
jo kankar charnon ko chhu le
jo kankar charnon ko chhu le
vo hi raah ho jaaye re
Ramji ke dvaare p
tora manva kyun ghabraaye re
laakh diin dukhiyaare praani
jag mein mukti paaye
he Raam ji ke dvaar se

n puuchhe vo gyaan kisi ki
n gun avgun
n gun avgun jaanche
vahi bhagat Bhagwan ko pyaara
jo har baani baanche
jo koyi shradda le ke aaye
jholi bharkar jaaye re
Raam ji ke dvaar se
tora manva
tora manva kyun ghabraaye re
laakh diin dukhiyaare praani
jag me mukti paaye
he Raam ji ke dvaar se

Stay Steadfast

This bhajan is difficult to put into a category. It is not addressed to a particular deity. It is about the self, about addressing inner turmoil. The worst thing that can happen to the self is if it loses its steadiness: it gives up, it is not ready to struggle any longer, it does not want to face unpleasant realities. What we learn here is an important lesson: our real strength is not physical stamina—how long we can walk; how much weight we can carry on our shoulders—it is the inner strength, the strength of our self, the source of our determination, the compass that shows us what our next destination is going to be.

O my Self, stay steadfast.
The one who is not moved by love
does not care who you love.
O my Self, stay steadfast.

No one has been able to tie down
life's sunshine that waxes and wanes.
Who can stop colour from shining?
Who can restrain the grandeur of beauty?
Why do you even think of doing this?
O my Self, stay steadfast.

If someone goes along with you, feel obliged.
We meet in life and death—put this dream aside.
No one dies with you; you die alone.
O my Self, don't lose your steadiness.
The one who is not moved by love
does not care who you love.
O my Self, stay steadfast.

Man Re Tu Kaahe N Dhiir Dhare

man re tu kaahe n dhiir dhare
vo nirmohi moh n jaane, jinka moh kare
man re tu kaahe n dhiir dhare

is jiivan ki charhti dhalti
dhuup ko kisne baandha
rang p kis ne pahre daale
ruup ko kis ne baandha
kaahe y jatan kare
man re tu kaahe n dhiir dhare

utna hi upkaar samajh koi
jitnaa saath nibha de
janma maran ka mel hai sapna
y sapna bisraa de
koi n sang mare
man re tu kaahe n dhiir dhare
vo nirmohi moh n jaane jinkaa moh kare
man re tu kaahe n dhiir dhare

Ishwar Allah are Your Names

This bhajan is very similar to 'Allah and Ishwar are Your Names'. It emphasizes the unity of all human beings and says no one is high- or low-born. All divisions on the basis of caste and race are wrong. If we are thinking about divisive issues, there is something wrong with our thinking. We should be focused on what unites us and not what divides us. Eventually, we should be judged by our actions and not our ego-driven claims about who we are.

Ishwar and Allah are your names.
Lord, give the gift of right thinking to all!

The world is your offspring.
Lord, give the gift of right thinking to all!

All those who live on this land,
they have grown up in your lap.
No one is lowly, no one is formidable.
Lord, give the gift of right thinking to all!
The whole world is your offspring.

Divisions of people based on caste and race
are false and meaningless.
In your estimation, all are equal.
Lord, give the gift of right thinking to all!

This life is precious. We can't put a price on it.
Life is not the true measure of a human's worth.
Everyone is known by his or her actions.

Ishwar and Allah are your names.
Lord, give the gift of right thinking to all!

The whole world is your offspring.
Lord, give the gift of right thinking to all!

Ishwar Allah Tere Naam

Ishwar Allah tere naam
sab ko sanmati de Bhagwaan

saara jag teri santaan
sab ko sanmati de Bhagwaan

is dharti par basnevaale
sab hain teri god ke paaley
koi niich n koi mahaan
sab ko sanmati de Bhagwaan
saara jag teri santaan

zaaton naslon ke bantvaare
jhuuth kahaayein tere dvaare
zaaton naslon ke bantvaare
jhuuth kahaayein tere dvaare
tere liye sab ek samaan
sab ko sanmati de Bhagwaan

janam ka koi mol nahien hai
janam manush ka tol nahien hai
karam se hai sab ki pehchaan
sab ko sanmati de Bhagwaan

Ishwar Allah tere naam
sab ko sanmati de Bhagwaan
saara jag teri santaan

Epilogue

Sahir passed away nearly forty years ago, but time has not diminished interest in his personality, his poetry, and his 'love affairs', as observed in social media, and there's an enduring public interest in his film lyrics. What is behind this undying attraction for him and his work? What is that unstoppable magic that draws us time and again to Sahir's poems and melodies? His book *Talkhiyaan* has appeared in dozens of Urdu and Hindi editions (both legal and pirated), and it is by far the largest-selling Urdu poetry book after *Divan-e Ghalib*. Compilations of his poetry have sold more than the books written by his progressive contemporaries like Majrooh, Majaz, Kaifi, Akhtar, and Jafri combined. What is behind this popular appeal that shows no sign of letting up? There are no easy answers.

I think there is the magic of Sahir's enigmatic personality. The choices he made in his life were far removed from the routine. He was a recluse, living alone in a big bungalow without any thought of starting his own family. His concept of family—he himself, his mother, and his two cousin sisters—was limiting. What would happen to his legacy when this family of four passed away? He never paid any attention to this.

He wrote highly appealing poetry that was deeply romantic, but it also had strong social, cultural, and political undertones. History has not been kind to progressives: The Soviet Union collapsed. China, once a bastion of communism, has become a one-party capitalistic state while nursing dreams of global domination. Nehruvian socialism in India has seen several dilutions through market-oriented reforms. Yet, hope for an equitable society still resonates. There is a powerful message in Sahir's poetry against the inequalities of wealth, maltreatment of women, exploitation of labour, and the threat of a more deadly nuclear war that still holds appeal, and his words give vivid expression to these injustices and fears in a most compelling poetic language. India's richest 1 per cent, according to an Oxfam report (2017), own 73 per cent of wealth. The position of women has improved over the past seventy years, but there's a huge scope for improvement. Child marriage is common, and access to education by young girls is limited. Incidents of rape and sexual assault are on the rise. In 2007, the Ministry of Women and Child Development reported the presence of over 3 million female sex workers in India, with about 36 per cent entering the trade before the age of eighteen. These statistics show the difficult task inherent in raising the status of women to be at par with men, something that all progressive poets strongly advocated. On the threat of a nuclear war, there are not only bad state actors globally who might use nuclear bombs to advance their interests, but regionally, India and Pakistan have the nuclear potential to completely destroy the whole subcontinent in case of a new armed conflict.

Although some people assert that Sahir separated himself from the literary world after he had achieved success as a film lyricist, he never agreed with this assessment. He treated literary pursuit as the core purpose of his life's journey. Every poem or ghazal that he wrote mirrored some facet of his own life. It was a tapestry into which he wove the fabric of his aspirations, his successes and his failures, and the bitter and sweet lessons of his life; there is no way to separate his biography from his poetry.

As mentioned before, Sahir's words often paint a gloomy picture of the world we live in, but we should not lose sight of his optimism. Although all progressive poets were optimistic in the sense that the revolution they expected to occur was supposed to be the natural cure for society's social and economic problems, Sahir, not being a member of the Communist Party, expected things to improve through social and political action outside the scope of a grand socialist revolution. For him, the day of a better tomorrow was not simply guesswork. It had to happen because people have the potential to create a better future for themselves. And this is something they are passionate about doing. Notice the words of a popular lyric from the 1958 movie *Phir Subha Hogi*:

That dawn will come one day—
when the veil of night will be lifted
from the dark times we live in.
When the clouds of suffering will dissolve
and an ocean of joyfulness will rise up.
When the sky will dance unchained
and the earth will sing wildly.
That dawn will come one day.
Waiting for that dawn since the beginning,
we have been living and dying.
In search of the nectar of that dawn,
we have been swallowing cups of poison.
That dawn will someday show mercy
to these hungry and thirsty souls.
That dawn will come one day.

voh sub-ha kabhi to aaye gi
in kaali sadiyon ke sar se jab raat ka aanchal dhalke ga
jab dukh ke baadal pighlein ge jab sach ka saaghar chhalke ga
jab ambar jhuum ke naache ga jab dharti naghme gaaye gi
voh sub-h kabhi to aaye gi
jis sub-h ki khaatir jug jug se ham sab mar mar kar jiite hain
jis sub-h ke amrit ki dhun mein ham zahr ke pyaale piite hain
in bhuuki pyaasi ruuhon par ik din to karam farmaaye gi
voh sub-h kabhi to aaye gi

Reading Sahir affects the reader on several levels—rational, intellectual, emotional, and psychological. No wonder readers can't get enough of Sahir!

A poet who consciously chose to call himself *sahir*—meaning a magician or a wizard—needs an aura of mystery; without this veil of the unknown and unexpected, his magic will cease to have any appeal.

Sahir's work is a feast in every sense of the word and, as someone who has enjoyed his poetry over the past several decades, I would say that there is great joy in this onslaught of lyrical thoughts and romantic overtures that his poetry offers.

The 20th century produced many outstanding Urdu poets, both modern and postmodern in their thinking, who rescued the ghazal from the fascinating, though totally unrealistic, themes of the previous centuries, and through their poems and ghazals brought new life to a poetic tradition that was losing its touch with reality. The relevant question is not whether Sahir was better than Faiz, Makhdoom, Majaz, Majrooh, Kaifi, or Jafri. They had much in common, but at the same time, each one of them had a distinctive style. Perhaps Faiz was the greatest of them all. But that does not minimize Sahir's importance. He is a poet of life who is in love with it despite all its bitterness and unpleasantness. Above all, he is a poet of peace, with concerns for the well-being of humanity. In a short poem titled 'I Love Life,' he wrote:

I love life.
I can't separate myself
from beauty.
The fire of passionate love
burns in my heartbeat even today.
And my heart is not doused yet.

Into the tapestry of life,
I'm busy adding colour.
I'm still occupied,
worrying about
the fate of the universe,
and my personal suffering
has not yet
come to an end.

The sacred word is dear to me.
Oppression is unpleasant.

Epilogue

Even today, my compact with the new age
is something that I shall keep.
I haven't died yet.

zindagi se uns hai
husn se lagaav hai
dharkano mein aaj bhi i'shq ka alaav hai
dil abhi bujha nahien

rang bhar raha huun main
khaaka-e hayaat mein
aaj bhi huun munhamik
fiqre kaaenaat mein
gham abhi luta nahien

harf-e haq aziz hai
zulm naagavaar hai
a'hd-e nau se aaj bhi
a'hd ustavaar hai
main abhi mara nahien

Acknowledgements

I would like to express my deepest gratitude to Professor Gopi Chand Narang, not only for his notable and consequential Foreword that sheds new light on Sahir as a poet and his relationships, but for the fact that he has been an illuminating guide, an enlightened teacher, and a worthy friend for the past several years. I have learnt a lot from him about the richness of Urdu literature, especially the complexities of the work of great poets like Ghalib as well as several modern and progressive poets, including Sahir. I would not have considered working on this book without his support and guidance.

It is impossible to create great written work without the support of one's family. My wife, Daler Aashna Deol, who is herself a poet, having published two collections of poetry in recent years, was my cheerleader as well as benevolent critic. Good writing takes time and it requires both appreciation and honest feedback; I would like to express my appreciation for her support and wise counsel. My thanks to my children and grandchildren for their love and affection. Writing often comes at the cost of spending less time with one's loved ones. I appreciate their patience and understanding.

I was influenced by Sahir's poetry when I was a teenager. The revolutionary tenor of his 'socialist' work, and his songs of unrequited love had special appeal to young people of my generation because of the social and cultural changes that were taking place in India and in other countries. Although the socialist revolution that the poet foresaw never materialized, the issues of social injustice, inequalities of wealth, protection of natural beauty, and mistreatment of women (some of Sahir's favourite themes) continue to be major debating points of today's politics, and that is the reason Sahir's words are as real to us today as they were when they were written. If there is one thing I learnt from Sahir that is of lasting value, it is his optimism. Despite all the hurdles human beings might face, there is a possibility for us to create a better world. It is my hope that this work reiterates his message in a way that is meaningful for today's young generation and for those adults who are in a position to influence thinking on social and cultural issues.

Select Bibliography

Abbas, K.A. 1985. 'Hamare Mulk Ke Maqbuul Tariin Shaa'yir'. In *Fan aur Shakhsiyat*, issue 17–18.

Ahmed, N.Z. (ed.) 2010. In *Adab Saaz*, issue 12–14.

Akhtar, Jan Nisar. 1985. 'Giiton Ka Rasiya'. In *Fan aur Shakhsiyat*, issue 17–18.

Ayubi, Mahmud. 1985. 'Anwar Bibi Ke Bhaijan'. *Fan aur Shakhsiyat*, issue 35–46.

Deol, Surinder. 2018. *The Treasure: A Modern Rendition of Ghalib's Lyrical Love Poetry*, 2nd edn. New Delhi: Partridge Publishing.

Dutt, Sabar and Sarvar Shafi, eds. 1985. In *Fan aur Shakhsiyat*, issue 17–18.

Farhat, W., ed. 1913. In *URDU* Quarterly Magazine, issue 2–4.

Gorakhpuri, Majnun. 1969. 'Jadeed Ghazal Pakistan aur Hindustan Mein'. In *Fanuun*.

Hirsch, Edward. 1999. *How to Read a Poem*. New York: Harcourt.

Jafri, Ali Sardar. 1985. 'Sahir Ka Shaayiraana Mizaj'. In *Fan aur Shakhsiyat*, issue 17–18.

Jalees, Ibrahim. 2010. 'Abdul Hayee Se Sahir Ludhianvi'. In *Adab Saaz*, issue 12–14.

Jamal, Mahmood, trans. 1986. *The Penguin Book of Modern Urdu Poetry*. Harmondsworth: Penguin Books.

Kapoor, Kanhaiya Lal. 2011. 'Phir Nazar Mein Phool Mehke'. In S. Taqi Abedi, *Faiz Fahmi*. Lahore: Reconer Publications.

Ludhianvi, Sahir. 1955. *Parchchaaiyaan*. Lahore: Maktaba Jadeed.

———. 1963. *Talkhiyaan*. Delhi: Star Publications.

———. 1964. *Gaata Jaaye Banjaara*. Delhi: Punjabi Pustak Bhandar.

———. 1973. *Aao K Koi Khwaab Bunein*. Delhi: Punjabi Pustak Bhandar.

———. 2003. *Kulliyaate Sahir*. Delhi: Kitabi Duniya.

Manwani, Akshay. 2013. *Sahir Ludhianvi: The People's Poet*. Delhi: HarperCollins, Kindle edition.

Narang, Gopi Chand. 2013. 'Sahir Ludhianvi aur Bhajan Ki Ma'anuyat'. In *URDU* Quarterly Magazine, issue 2–4.

Narang, Gopi Chand. 2014. *Ghalib: Ma'ni Aafrini Jadilyati Vaza' Shunyata aur Sheriyaat*. New Delhi: Sahitya Akademi.

———. 2017. *Ghalib: Innovative Meanings and the Ingenious Mind*, trans. Surinder Deol. New Delhi: Oxford University Press.

Nayyar, Rehman, ed. *Beesvi Sadi*, issue 12, vol. 44.

Neruda, Pablo. 1986. *100 Love Sonnets*, trans. Stephen Tapscott. Austin: University of Texas Press.

Oliver, Mary. 1998. *Rules for the Dance*. New York: Houghton Mifflin Company.

Pritam, Amrita. 1985. '*Yaadon Ke Lams*'. In *Fan aur Shakhsiyat*, issue 17–18.

———. 2008. *Rasiidi Ticket*. Delhi: Kitabghar Prakashan.

———. 2010. '*Kore Kaghaz Ki Daastaan*'. In *Adab Saaz*, issue 12–14.

Rahi, Ahmad. 2010. '*Ek Diya Aur Bujha*'. In *Adab Saaz*, issue 12–14.

Trilok, Uma. 2006. *Amrita-Imroze: A Love Story*. New Delhi: Penguin Books India.

Varma, Chander and Salman Abid. 2014. *Main Sahir Huun*. Delhi: Takhleeqkar Publishers.

Zaheer, Sajjad. 1985. '*Phuulon Se Ladi Hui Champa Ki Khushboo*'. In *Fan aur Shakhsiyat*, issue 17–18.

Index

About the Author

Surinder Deol served as a programme manager and a senior specialist at the World Bank in Washington, DC. Prior to this, he held a senior managerial position at the Industrial Development Bank of India (IDBI) and as director of the Management Development Institute (MDI) in Gurgaon. Earlier, his areas of interest included cross-cultural negotiations and leadership development, and he published books and facilitated several international seminars and symposia on these issues. His interest in Ghalib's poetry, a passion from his early years, led him to translate *Divan-e Ghalib* in free verse, which was published as *The Treasure: A Modern Rendition of Ghalib's Lyrical Love Poetry*, in 2014. A new revised and expanded edition of the book appeared in 2018. He has also written the novel *Endless Life* (2012), and the collection of poems *A Moment in the Universe* (2006). More recently, he translated Gopi Chand Narang's classic study of Ghalib's poetics into English, published as *Ghalib: Innovative Meanings and the Ingenious Mind* (2017). He lives in Potomac, Maryland, USA, with his wife, Daler Aashna Deol.